Cornwall Walking on the level

Norman and June Buckley

Published by Sigma Leisure – an imprint of
Sigma Press, Stobart House, Pontyclerc, Penybanc Road
Ammanford, Carmarthenshire SA18 3HP

British Library Cataloguing in Publication Data

A CIP record for this book is available from the British Library

ISBN: 978-1-85058-895-5

Typesetting and Design by: Sigma Press, Ammanford, Carms

Maps: © Bute Cartographics

Photographs: © June Buckley

Cover photographs: © Norman and June Buckley
Main picture: Porthleven
Left to right: *Helford; Valency Valley;; The Cheesewring; First and Last House, Land's End*

Printed by: Berforts Group Ltd, Stevenage

Disclaimer: The information in this book is given in good faith and is believed to be correct at the time of publication. Care should always be taken when walking in hill country. Where appropriate, attention has been drawn to matters of safety. The author and publisher cannot take responsibility for any accidents or injury incurred whilst following these walks. Only you can judge your own fitness, competence and experience. Do not rely solely on sketch maps for navigation: we strongly recommend the use of appropriate Ordnance Survey (or equivalent) maps.

Contents

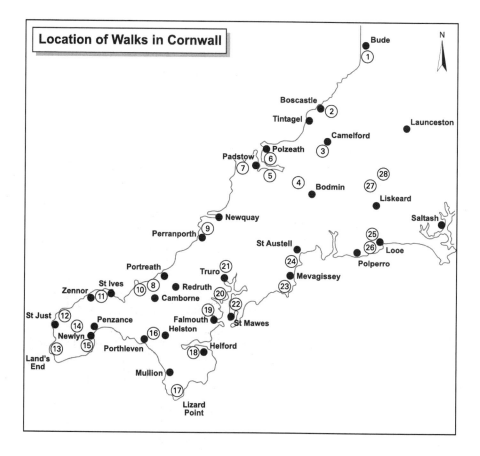

Location of Walks in Cornwall

N

Bude
①

Boscastle
②

Tintagel

Camelford
Launceston

Polzeath
③

Padstow
⑥

⑦   ⑤

④   Bodmin

㉘

㉗   Liskeard

Saltash

Newquay

Perranporth   ⑨

St Austell   ㉕

㉖   Looe

Portreath

Truro   ㉑

㉔

St Ives   ⑩   ⑧   Redruth

㉓   Mevagissey

Polperro

Zennor   ⑪

Camborne   ⑳

St Just   ⑫   ⑲   ㉒

St Mawes

Penzance   ⑭   Falmouth

Newlyn   ⑯   Helston

⑬   ⑮   Porthleven

⑱   Helford

Land's
End

Mullion

⑰

Lizard
Point

Introduction

Many visitors to Cornwall are likely to include countryside and, particularly, coastal walking as part of their holiday activity. The range is great; there are strong walkers who will spend several weeks hard walking on the superb South West Coast Path, perhaps taking several holidays spread over time to achieve the total distance. At the other extreme are those who just want to park the car or (preferably) get off the bus and stroll to some worthwhile destination, be it a cliff top viewpoint, a delectable harbour or cove or merely a well-known inn.

This seventh volume of the well-established *Level Walks* series offers twenty-eight walks aimed between the above extremes, generally intended for those who, for whatever reason, want interesting walks at the less strenuous end of the scale.

Level Walks is not, of course to be taken literally. It means that the first criterion in selecting a route is limitation of the ascent which, for many people, often rules out otherwise good walks. The acceptability of any route is primarily determined by the aggregate ascent, (with a guideline of approximately 125m (410ft). Whether that ascent is spread throughout the route or occurs in one long climb, the gradients and the nature of the walking surface are also taken into account.

Most of the previous *Level Walks* books have been in distinctly mountainous areas such as the Lake District and North Wales, where the concept is of particular value in helping walkers to find routes among the mountains without having to climb any of those mountains. In Cornwall there are no real mountains but many of the popular walks, particularly those including the South West Coast Path, have a great deal of rise and fall and, overall, are too demanding for the more casual walker. Many sections of the Coast Path are, however, included in this book but have been carefully selected to combine maximum enjoyment with minimum effort in each case. The walks are generally quite short because of the difficulty of finding longer routes in which the aggregate ascent is within the guidelines. It is also assumed that those with a preference for 'level' walks will be unlikely to want really long walks. Most are circular but in six cases the recommended return is by bus or train. In addition to the coast path, the routes are diversified by the use of disused railway lines, moorland and agricultural tracks and some woodland.

Supplementing the vital statistics, there is careful selection of starting/finishing places, refreshment opportunities and recommended maps, together with the description of scenery and places along the way, all summarised at the start of each walking route.

For such generally easy walks, no particular recommendations are made concerning clothing, footwear or the carrying of food and drink. Suffice it to say that experienced walkers would be unlikely to tackle sections of the Coast Path or Bodmin Moor without appropriately strong footwear, preferably boots.

Walk 1: Bude

As a holiday resort Bude is one of the quieter little towns, well placed at the north-east corner of the county, altogether pleasant, with good beaches and an excellent tourist information centre.

Most notable is the Bude Canal, built in the 1820s with the ambitious object of providing a waterway across Cornwall, linking the Atlantic Ocean and the English Channel. In the event the canal reached only as far as Launceston, with the aid of several unusual inclined planes. The tub boats had wheels on which they were hauled up and down on rails. Sand was carried inland, for improvement of the predominantly acid soils, with assorted produce travelling in the other direction. After the arrival of the London and South Western Railway in the 1890s, the canal closed to traffic. The sea lock and the section inland from Bude have been extensively renovated, the towpath ('Bude Heritage Trail') now forming an attractive walk, with modern sculptures along the way.

The Bude-Stratton Museum is situated in the 19th century castle, close to the canal.

This is truly a walk for all abilities, involving the canal, part of the disused railway branch line and the town's beach. Boots are not necessary.

Distance	4½km (2¾ miles)
Ascent	Negligible
Start/car parking	Large pay and display car park with public conveniences behind Bude main beach, grid reference 205065
Refreshments	Inns and cafés in Bude, including the Castle Tea Room
Map	Ordnance Survey Explorer 111, Bude, Boscastle and Tintagel, 1:25,000

The Walk

From the car park head towards the beach, but fork left through a gap before reaching the modern lifeboat station. Cross about 150m of loose sand to reach a footbridge.

1. Turn left to cross the bridge, over the River Neet. To the right is the wall of the great sea lock which regulated the access to the Bude Canal, vital for the town's former importance. Go up the steps on the right to reach canal level. Turn left along a hard-surfaced footpath, with the canal on the right. Pass the low mound with the (19th century) castle and the Castle Tea Room. Stay close to the canal to reach the town's main road.

2. Cross over the road to a little gate giving access to a canal-side path, again hard surfaced. Pass the prominent modern Tourist Information Centre and the first of a series of modern sculptures. Pass a bird-watching hide with views over Bude Marshes Nature Reserve. Ignore a footbridge on the left, continuing by the side of the canal. There are occasional seats along the way.

3. Reach a very minor road, close to a bridge. Do not cross the bridge; turn left to walk along the road, crossing Rodd's Bridge over the River Neet. Immediately before the abutments of a dismantled railway bridge, turn left to follow a hard surfaced cycle and

Sea lock, Bude Canal

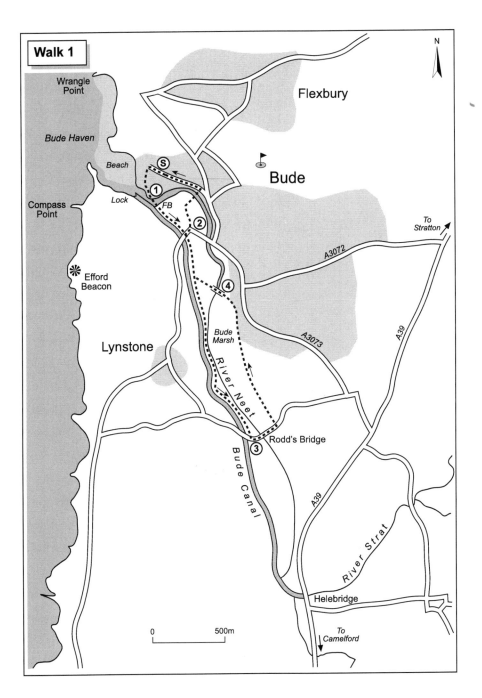

walkway, following the line of the former railway, on its embankment to the right. At a signposted junction keep right for 'Bude' to continue along the edge of the Marshes nature reserve. At the next fork go left, along an unsurfaced path with a little sign 'Bude Canal Trails, Bude Valley'.

Sculpture, Bude Canal

4. On reaching a surfaced track turn left to cross a bridge over the river, pass an information board and rejoin the outward route, bearing right to return towards the town centre. From this point either re-use the outward route or cross the road to Ergue-Gaberic Way, to the left of the post office. In 10m turn right into a cul-de-sac road. Fork left in 25m, pass the Central Methodist Church, cross a footbridge over the River Neet and turn left to return to the car park.

Walk 2: Boscastle

The most characteristic feature of Boscastle is the long creek with steep-sided hills on each side, providing a narrow little port. At certain states of the tide a well-known 'blow hole' is evident at the seaward end of the creek. Inland, the village is quietly attractive, with the site of a Norman castle, former mill, shops, inn and cafés. Two substantial streams converge here and there was serious flooding in 2004, with a great deal of damage to property. Boscastle has long been a popular tourist destination, with a comprehensive visitor centre.

A little more than two miles from Boscastle, accessed by the road towards Bude (B3263) and a narrow lane, the remotely sited St Juliot's Church is worth a visit, with a churchyard containing three ancient granite crosses. In 1872 the building was restored; the architect was the young Thomas Hardy who did a generally competent job. Of

St Juliot's Church, near Boscastle

Distance	(New Mill) 4km (2½ miles)
Ascent	Negligible
Start/car parking	Large pay and display car park in Boscastle, grid reference 100913
Refreshments	Cobweb Inn, Pilchard Cellar Tea Rooms (National Trust) and other cafés in Boscastle
Map	Ordnance Survey Explorer 111, Bude, Boscastle and Tintagel, 1:25,000

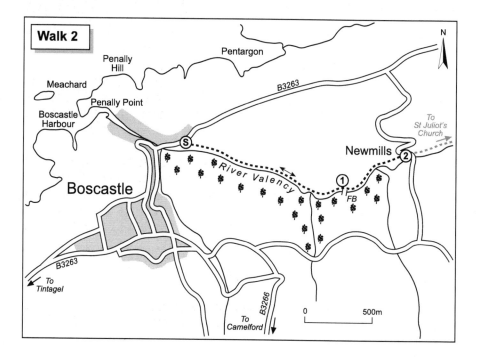

Boscastle

particular interest is a window with etched glass. Hardy first met his future (first) wife Emma here; she was related to the Vicar. There is a charming story of she and Thomas searching in the stream below the church for a drinking glass lost in the water during a picnic.

The route of the walk is entirely within the quiet and beautiful wooded valley of the Valency, one of the two streams/rivers converging at Boscastle, an out and back route terminating at New Mill with a possible extension to reach St Juliot's Church. The track is very easy to the bridge at point 1, and is still good but a little more sporting between the bridge and New Mill.

The Walk

Walk through or beside the car park to the far end. Go through a gate and follow a well-used track, basically level along the valley of the

River Valency, soon in attractive diversified woodland. Pass the remnants of a weir, from where a leat on the far side of the river carried the water to power the former mill in the middle of the village. Pass stepping stones across the river before reaching a footbridge with a nearby seat.

1. Do not cross; continue as the path becomes a little more sporting, with a few steps and possibly some mud, but still relatively easy.

2. Reach New Mills, with a few buildings, as the path joins a surfaced road. The level walk ends here.

To continue to St Juliot's Church go down the drive leading to Elm Cottage, forking left at a signpost in a few metres to rise steadily, crossing several fields on the way to the church. The '¼ mile' suggested by the signpost is actually ¾ mile.

Walk 3: Camelford

An unpretentious little place with one narrow main street, unfortunately the main A39, Camelford is an ancient market town, with a 13th century Royal Charter. Camelford is close to Bodmin Moor, but is hardly a moorland town. Until 1832, two members were sent to Parliament – very much a 'rotten borough'. The name is derived from the strategic crossing place of the upper reaches of the River Camel, now an unremarkable bridge. From 1893, the North Cornwall railway line passed close to the town on its way to Wadebridge and Padstow. This line, alas, is now long gone. There are still several shops, inns and cafés in what is, overall, a pleasant place.

The circuit, which includes lengths of the designated Moorland Walk, combines a part of the delightful valley of the River Camel with agricultural land close to the higher ground of Bodmin Moor. The splendid Rough Tor is a dominant feature. Good paths, minor roads and traverses of pathless fields are all included; there are several

Camelford

Distance	8½km (5¼ miles)
Ascent	80m (263ft)
Start/car parking	Large free car park at north end of Camelford's main street, close to the church, grid reference 108839
Refreshments	Inns and cafés in Camelford
Map	Ordnance Survey Explorer 109, Bodmin Moor, 1:25,000

stiles, some of them old and traditional, and muddy areas are likely. The ascent is divided broadly into three sections, two of which are moderately steep.

An interesting feature is the Advent Church of St Athwenna, remotely situated in the fields to the south of Trethin.

The Walk

From the car park turn right to walk along the main street. Pass a signpost which includes 'Moorlands Walk', cross the River Camel, pass the Town Hall and the Darlington Inn.

1. In a further 40m turn left to descend an alleyway signposted 'public footpath to the river and Advent Church'. A charming path beside the infant River Camel heads straight into the countryside, crossing the river on footbridges several times and passing the town's sewage disposal works. There are gates before a surfaced lane is reached, with a bridge (Fenteroon) to the left.

2. Turn right here for the first of the ascents, moderately steeply up the road. After a left bend, as the gradient eases, turn left at a 'public footpath' signpost. Go through a little gate and follow a clear path with a field fence on the right. Go over a waymarked old stile. After the next (high) old stile, descend through woodland as the path angles down the valley side. Ignore a stile on the right as

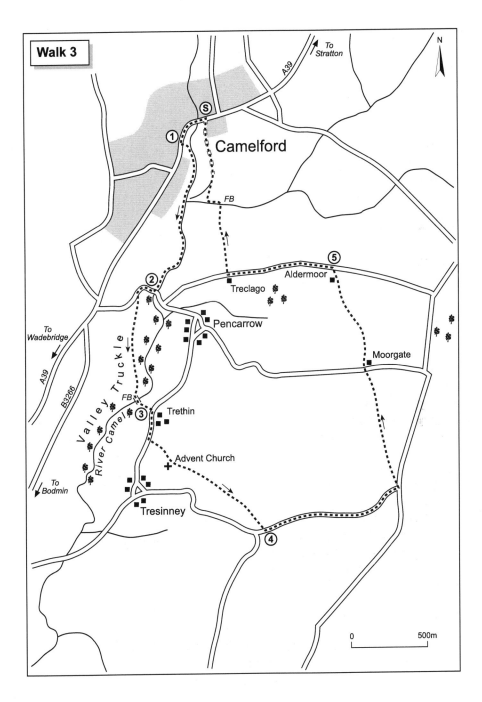

Walk 3

To
Stratton

A39

N

Camelford

FB

Treclago

Aldermoor

Pencarrow

To
Wadebridge

Moorgate

A39

B3266

Valley Truckle

River Camel

FB

Trethin

Advent Church

To
Bodmin

Tresinney

0　　　　　500m

the path leaves the woodland through a gap to cross a rough meadow, rich in bramble. Cross the River Camel on a waymarked footbridge, followed by a steep little ascent up the bank on the left. Pass a waymark on a post and keep to the cattle-churned edge of a rising meadow.

3. Go over a signposted stile at the top of the meadow to reach a surfaced lane. Turn right to pass the impressive Trethin farmstead. Ten metres after the farm entrance turn left over a waymarked stile. Cross a stream on a mini clapper bridge to a stile before rising across a field to the now visible Advent Church. Go over a stile to enter the churchyard. Leave the churchyard by a gate and stile at the left corner (take care here, there are several footpaths), ignoring the direction indicated by the waymark. Cross a large field, bearing a little to the right to reach a stile about half way along the far boundary. There are three stiles in close sequence; continue to another stile in 60m. Continue to rise gently across the next field, following the direction indicated by the waymark to a stile in the top right corner. Go over a triple stile on the right in 100m, then

Rough Tor, Near Camelford

continue diagonally left across the next field to reach a double stile 15m to the left of the top right corner.

4. Go over and join a surfaced lane, turning left to rise very gently, with views to the higher parts of Bodmin Moor, including Rough Tor. Pass the entrance to Quoitcombe Farm before descending to Watergate Farm. Turn left immediately before a bridge and road junction ('public footpath' sign). Go over a double stile and along a path initially with paving slabs, beside a stream. There are more stiles before the barely visible path ascends gently to the left across a meadow to a waymarked stile. From the stile follow the direction indicated by the waymark to head towards Moorgate Farm. Go through a farm gate between buildings to reach a lane. Across the lane is a 'public footpath' sign. Go through a gateway to the left of the sign and pass to the left of a farm building For the next half mile, the route crosses several fields, without visible paths but heading for an assortment of gates and stiles, descending gently. The general direction is a little to the west of north, heading just to the right of a distant residential area to reach a stony track leading to Aldermoor Farm.

5. Pass the farm. Turn left to follow the access road, an attractive lane, as far as Treclago Farm. At the farm turn right, rising a little along a broad, unsurfaced track. Go straight ahead at a cross tracks, past a muddy area to reach a gate. After the gate keep to the right across a descending meadow to reach a waymarked gate, stile and footbridge. Cross and bear left; go over a stile and turn right to ascend along the edge of a steep meadow to a gate. Go through, join a surfaced lane, turn right and follow the lane, at first uphill but then gently downhill to join the main road through Camelford. Go straight across the road to return to the car park.

Walk 4: Wadebridge and the Camel Trail

A former medieval port on the tidal reaches of the River Camel, Wadebridge has evolved into a 'working' town, pleasant enough but without particular distinction. There are inns, cafés, shops and tourist information. The long seventeen-arched bridge is of the late 15th century, with widening in the mid 19th century and the 1960s. The John Betjeman Centre, in the former railway station building, has memorabilia of the former Poet Laureate who had a family home in this part of North Cornwall. There is also a café.

The outline history of the railway is included in walk 5, together with its partial conversion into the Camel Trail.

Burlawn is a scattered village on the hillside above the Camel estuary. There are a few pleasant old cottages and two chapel buildings but nothing of particular distinction.

Distance	8km (5 miles)
Ascent	105m (345ft)
Start/car parking	Roadside lay-by spaces at the far end of the cul-de-sac Guineaport Road, grid reference 995719. From the town centre head south-east along the main street; opposite the cinema turn left to follow Guineaport Road to the end, passing the John Betjeman Centre at the former railway station. Alternatively, use a town centre car park and walk to the end of Guineaport Road. Out and back this adds almost one mile to the overall distance
Refreshments	Choice in Wadebridge
Map	Ordnance Survey Explorer 106, Newquay and Padstow, 1:25,000

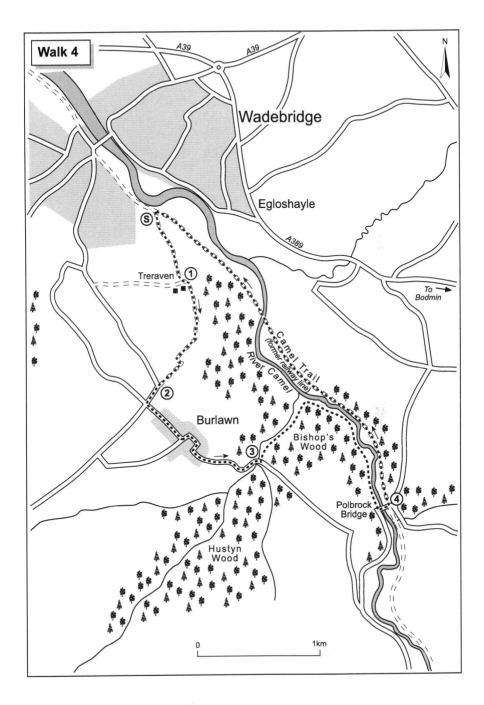

For the purpose of this walk, a section of the Camel Trail is combined with footpaths and a rural lane to provide a varied circuit. At the start of the route there is a quite prolonged ascent but the gradient is never unduly steep and the only problem underfoot is likely to be mud.

The Walk

Start at the point where a signposted footpath to Treraven leaves the Camel Trail, close to the river. Take the footpath, initially a hard surfaced road, forking right, uphill. In a few metres the road bends to the right; go straight ahead on a broad track, rising steadily. The track soon narrows, reaching a waymarked gate with a 'permissive access to Treraven Farm' sign. Continue along the right edge of a field, with views across the River Camel to Wadebridge suburbs, to reach another gate and a lane between high hedges, still rising gently, with mud likely.

Walkers on the Camel Trail

Railway locomotives, Bodmin

1. At a signposted crossing of tracks, by the access to Treraven Farm, turn left, bearing right at once to reach a Gaia Trust information board. Pass the farm (behind trees on the right) and continue the route along a sunken lane. At a farm gate there is a fine view over Wadebridge. There are sharp bends in each direction before a minor road is reached at an isolated house, 'Trig the Wheel'.

2. Turn left to walk by the side of the road. At a junction, in 150m, turn left to enter Burlawn, a village spread along this road. Pass the 'Old Chapel', the adjacent 'School House' and a terrace of attractive old cottages before the road descends steeply to leave the village. There is an old well on the left, then Gamekeeper's Cottage on the right before the former Hustyn Mill is reached at the bottom. Cross the stream which powered the mill; in times of flood use the roadside footbridge.

3. Ignore a footpath on the left; in a further 10m turn left at a broad entrance to Bishop's Wood (Forestry Commission). The forest

roadway provides a firm-surfaced level route through the predominantly coniferous but attractive woodland of a side valley, which descends to join the valley of the River Camel, bending to the right as the main valley is reached. Keep straight ahead at any junction. Pass a small picnic area before joining a minor road. Turn left to cross the river on Polbrock Bridge.

4. In a further 40m turn left to descend, either by steps or a steep path, to the trackbed of the former railway line – now the Camel Trail. Turn left to follow the trail back to the starting point. The Trail is mostly attractively wooded and is never far from the river. A former halt, Shooting Range Platform, is passed before the Trail crosses a bridge over the river and reaches the parking area.

Walk 5: Padstow and Wadebridge

Even before the arrival of Rick Stein and other celebrity caterers, Padstow had long been a popular resort, based on a substantial fishing port situated on the estuary of the River Camel. The little town is a pleasing jumble of narrow streets, with buildings in many styles, some of considerable antiquity. There are shops, inns and cafés in profusion and, despite the huge area necessarily occupied by car parks, much of the original character is still evident. There is a Tourist Information Centre by the harbour.

In 1899, the London and South Western Railway arrived, much increasing the number of visitors; for many years, until 1964, the little station was daily the final destination of the Atlantic Coast Express, a through train from London (Waterloo). All passenger services ceased in 1967 but the original station building can still be identified beside the entrance to a huge car park.

Wadebridge is very different, a former medieval port and a 'working' town focussed on the tidal River Camel, which brought sizeable sailing ships to wharves and quays, largely on the south bank. There are shops, inns and tourist information. The first bridge across the river, with seventeen arches, was built late in the 15th century. This long

Distance	9km (5½ miles)
Ascent	Negligible
Start/car parking	Large pay and display car park on the site of he former railway station, Padstow, grid reference 922749
Refreshments	Inns and cafés at Wadebridge and Padstow
Map	Ordnance Survey Explorer 106, Newquay and Padstow, 1:25,000

bridge has survived, having been widened twice, once in the mid 19th century and, latterly, in the 1960s.

A railway was constructed from Wadebridge to Wenford Bridge on Bodmin Moor, with a branch to Bodmin, in 1834, one of the earliest steam railways in the country and for many years totally detached from any other line. Minerals and granite from the Moor were taken to Wadebridge for onward shipment.

It was not until 1888 that the Great Western Railway built a connection from its main line at Bodmin Road (now Bodmin Parkway) to Bodmin, with running powers over part of the earlier line. In 1895 the London and South Western Railway, owners of the Wadebridge to Wenford Bridge line for many years, at last connected it to their main system by building a line across North Cornwall from Launceston.

The preserved Bodmin and Wenford Railway now operates largely steam-hauled services on part of the line to a seasonal timetable, as a visitor attraction based on the former Bodmin General Station.

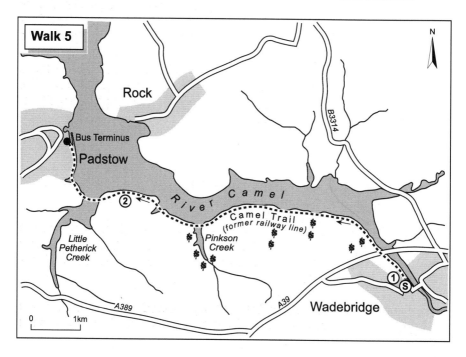

Bridge on Camel Trial

The remainder of the former line has been developed as The Camel Trail, for use by walkers, cyclists and horse riders. This Trail has become very popular, an easy-walking, level, route with high scenic attraction. The section used for the present walk is by the side of the estuary of the River Camel. The route is set out as a linear walk from a start in Wadebridge; obviously it can be reversed if preferred. The 555 bus provides a convenient link between the former station site at Padstow and the bus station at Wadebridge.

The Walk

At Padstow the bus stop is marked by a shelter at the car park entrance/exit.

At Wadebridge there is a choice of bus stop. Either use the bus station and walk back along the main road to the roundabout, below the Lidl store, or leave the bus at a stop 200m before the roundabout, above the Lidl store, close to the fire station.

1. The start of the Camel Trail is well signposted, close to prominent bicycle hire depots. Set off along the broad trail, initially hard

surfaced, heading towards the
quite elegant viaduct which
carries the Wadebridge by-pass
road across the Camel Valley.
The river is close on the right.
Pass the sewage disposal works;
the trail now loses its tarmac
surface and there is a 'Padstow
5' sign. Pass through a deep
cutting, one of several on the
Trail. There are occasional seats
along the way. Pass a bird-
watching hide and under a
stone bridge, wide enough to

Camel Trail Sign

accommodate a double track railway line. Reach the remains of a
quarry, with spoil heaps and a modern house to the left. There is a
'Padstow 3' sign. Cross Pinkson Creek on a low embankment and
pass above a small car park. Cross Oldtown Cove on an
embankment, followed by a cutting with the sides netted to prevent
falling rocks. Padstow comes into view as does Rock, across the
estuary, and Stepper Point in the far distance.

2. At Pentreath Point is a monument commemorating the
   establishment of the Camel Trail and a picnic area. Pass a vehicular
   crossing point before reaching the long metal bridge spanning
   Little Petherick Creek. The end of the trail, at the former railway
   station, is only a little further.

Walk 6: Rock and Daymer Bay

Facing Padstow across the estuary of the River Camel, the quiet village of Rock, with its wide sandy beaches, has become distinctly fashionable in recent years. Using the ferry service across the water, it is a popular destination for excursions from Padstow. The coast between Rock, Daymer Bay and Trebetherick is largely of sandy dunes, with the sharp little Brea Hill providing contrast. Much of the land between the settlements is occupied by the St Enodoc Golf Course.

This was an area beloved of Sir John Betjamen, who is buried at St Enodoc Church. This isolated church, with its twisted Norman tower, has a history of the building being almost covered by wind-

John Betjeman's Grave

Distance	5km (3 miles)
Ascent	Low tide 60m (197ft) High tide at Brea Hill 80m (263ft)
Start/car parking	Pay and display car park at Rock, grid reference 929768
Refreshments	Inn and café at Rock, facing the Camel Estuary
Map	Ordnance Survey Explorer 106, Newquay and Padstow, 1:25,000

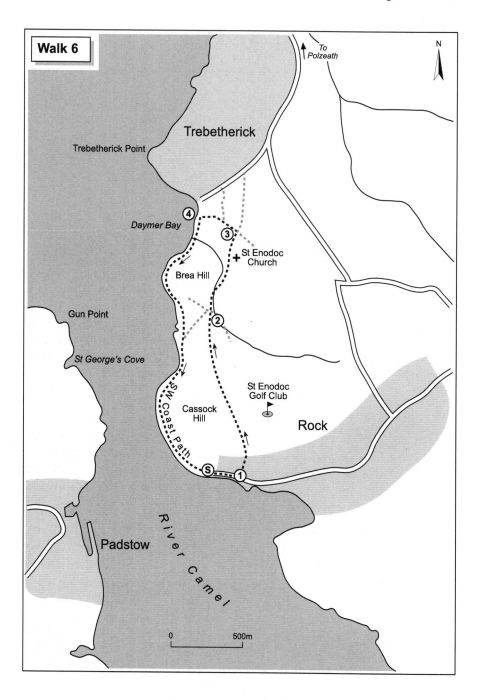

blown sand on many occasions over the centuries. It is now protected by a dense tamarisk hedge. Inside, despite 19th century restoration, a cut-down medieval screen and a Norman font are still evident.

This comparatively short, circular, route is attractively varied and has no problems underfoot. The section across the golf course is clearly marked, whilst the return, largely along the beach at low tide or across the flank of Brea Hill at high tide, is straightforward and undemanding.

The Walk

Walk back along the road for approximately 300m, passing the inn and the café. There are good views across the estuary to Padstow, seen at its best at this range.

1. Turn left at a minor road signposted to St Enodoc Golf Club, rising quite steeply for the major ascent of the circuit. Immediately before the entrance to the golf club car park turn left along a surfaced roadway. In 15m turn right to follow a little path, with a notice giving walkers advice about crossing the golf course. The scrubby vegetation is varied, soon giving way to the more open golf course. The well-used path initially keeps to the left of the course, with very clear white stone markers.

2. Turn right at a junction, cross a trolley way to a white stone opposite and continue, heading towards the Polzeath built-up area. Reach a tarmac road. Turn left for a few metres then bear right, downhill, at a waymarked post to reach a solid stone bridge crossing an attractive little stream. Turn left at once to follow the markers, quite close to the stream; St Enodoc's Church is in view ahead. The path keeps to the left of the church; to visit, go up to the right on the nearside of the church enclosure. The poet's grave, with simple headstone is found on the right immediately after entering the churchyard. There are seats from which the church and its lovely setting, including Brea Hill, the estuary and Stepper Point can be admired.

3. At a waymarked fork, 100m after the church, bear left; there are more white stones. Go straight ahead at a junction, to leave the golf course and descend a sandy slope to reach the beach at Daymer

Bay. About 200m to the right is a car park with public conveniences.

4. Turn left at the beach to walk towards the shapely hump of Brea Hill. At low tide it is possible to walk along the beach all the way back to Rock. At other times, cross the little stream at the foot of Brea Hill (there is a hardly necessary bridge). Ascend the sandy slope and follow the clear path to the right, around the flank of the hill. After the hill, go to the right at a fork, with a waymark on a post. The track, one of several across this sand dune country, heads south, just a little up and down but always clear. Reach the back of a sandy beach. Except at high tide stay with the beach back to Rock; at high tide go up to the left to find a track. At Rock leave the beach up a boat launching ramp. At the top is a signpost 'coast path, car park and toilets 40 yards'. Follow this, steeply uphill, to return.

St Enodoc's Church

Walk 7: Harlyn Bay and Trevose Head

Flanked by the broad sands of Constantine and Harlyn Bays, the bold headland of Trevose is a superb section of the north coast, which includes a lighthouse. Mother Ivey's Bay has splendid rock and beach scenery, but inland a static caravan site does nothing to enhance the landscape. Harlyn has a historic burial ground.

Combining a fine length of the South West Coast Path with an inland connecting link, this circuit has a total ascent which approaches the limit for 'level' walkers. In addition, there are several stiles. However, none of the gradients is steep and the various tracks are all good.

Distance	9km (5½ miles)
Ascent	120m (394ft)
Start/car parking	Large (pay in season) car park at Harlyn Bay, grid reference 880755
Refreshments	Harlyn Inn. Hotel at Constantine Bay
Map	Ordnance Survey Explorer 106, Newquay and Padstow, 1:25,000

The Walk

Facing the sea, turn left to walk along the back of the beach, bearing left to rise to the road immediately before Harlyn Bridge. Cross the bridge; in 10m turn right at a coast path signpost – 'Treyarnon Bay 4½ miles' – bearing left to walk along the back of the beach for about 400m.

1. Look out for a flight of steps with a waymarked post part way up. Ascend, then turn right at the top to continue along the coast path. The views back over Harlyn Bay are superb; the prominent offshore island is Gulland Rock. Go over two ancient (slightly awkward) stiles and pass a substantial dwelling ('The Cellars'). The ascent

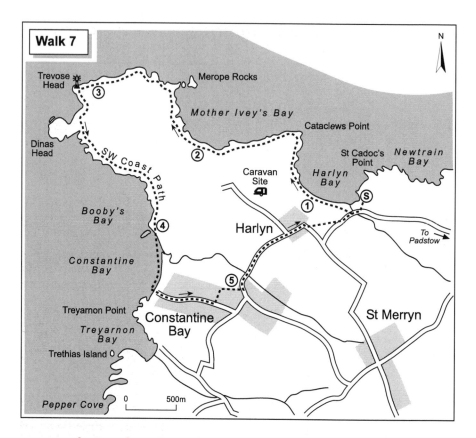

towards Cataclews Point is comparatively gentle but the views of a static caravan site are unfortunate. Close to the caravan site, descend then ascend flights of steps above a sandy beach.

2. Join a concrete track, turning left. In 15m fork back right to a kissing gate and continue along the path. Pass behind a bungalow, soon rising steadily, with Padstow lifeboat station in view across Mother Ivey's Bay. Go over two stiles before reaching a surfaced road. Turn left at the sign then, in 10m, turn right at a waymarked easy stile. Continue to rise gently, crossing the road leading to the lifeboat station, with a stile on each side. Continue towards Trevose Head, now in wilder countryside with abundant gorse and an ancient field boundary wall on the left. The track bears to the left as Trevose Head lighthouse comes into view.

3. Pass above the lighthouse; there is a communications station at the highest point, above to the left. Join a surfaced roadway to pass above Stinking Cove and reach a car park. Turn sharp right along the near edge of the car park to descend to a stile on the left in 70m. Turn left at the stile to follow a broad easy path heading gently downhill towards Constantine Bay. Pass an impressive blow-hole ('Round Hole') and several seats to reach a kissing gate. Pass a large isolated house, then Booby's Bay and along the edge of a golf course.

4. Descend steps to reach the beach at Constantine Bay. Walk along the beach, heading for the lifeguard hut. Go up the obvious ramp, bearing left to a car park and public conveniences. Continue along the beach access road, gently uphill. In a little under half a mile turn left at a 'public footpath' sign to follow a broad lane. After passing the last house, the lane becomes a footpath, soon joining another track. Turn right, rising gently along a pleasant path between hedges.

Harlyn Bay

5. Join a road close to the club house of the Trevose Golf and Country
   Club. Turn very sharp left, keeping the club house on the right, and
   follow the minor road, soon rising gently to reach a road junction
   at Harlyn hamlet. Bear a little to the right to follow 'Harlyn Bay ¼',
   downhill. In about 200m turn left at a signposted footpath, go over
   a stile and cross a cultivated field on a good path heading directly
   to dwellings at Harlyn Bay. Join a residential road, bearing right to
   join the main road. Turn left at the junction to pass the Harlyn Inn,
   cross Harlyn Bridge and bear left into the car park.

Harlyn Bay

Walk 8: North Cliffs and Tehidy Country Park

The cliff scenery of this part of the North Cornwall coast, immediately to the south-west of Portreath, is a mixture of unstable shale and sandstone, with offshore islands, spectacular formations and iron age forts.

Inland, Tehidy Country Park is a well sheltered, predominantly wooded area, formerly the extensive private estate of Tehidy Park House.

With the exception of the path along the edge of the field, after point 3, all tracks used for this circuit are very good; the ascent at the end of the walk is quite prolonged but not unduly steep.

Distance	5¼ km (3¼ miles)
Ascent	65m (213ft)
Start/car parking	North Cliffs car park on edge of Tehidy Country Park, accessed by B3301, south-west from Portreath, grid reference 640438
Refreshments	Polcrowjy Tea Gardens at Coombe
Map	Ordnance Survey Explorer 104, Redruth and St Agnes, 1:25,000

The Walk

From the car park walk back to the road. Turn right, along the roadside for about 100m.

1. Turn left down a public byway signposted '300 yards to the coast path'.

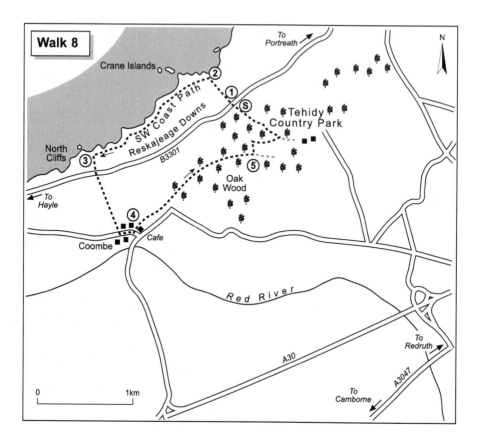

2. At a car park turn left to follow the coast path, almost level, for a little more than one mile, with fine views out to sea. To the right, near the start, is the residue of an iron age fort, Crane Castle. There are great swathes of heather and the occasional view of sandstone cliffs along the way. At Greenbank Cove there is visible evidence of cliff collapse and land slippage.

3. At another informal car park, behind Deadman's Cove, turn left, cross the road to a signposted (easy) stile, and take a narrow path down the left edge of a large field. Much of this path is rather overgrown. At the bottom go through a gate to join a minor road at the hamlet of Coombe. Turn left for about 130m.

4. Turn left again along a track, initially hard surfaced, to enter the Tehidy Country Park. On the right is the entrance to the Polcrowjy Tea Gardens. The track continues as a broad forest roadway, rising very gently through mature and diversified woodland for a little more than one mile. Part way along there is a sign pointing towards the 'Oak Wood' on the right. Ignore this.

5. As the track forks, bear left, uphill, soon reaching a T-junction. Turn left, still rising, to reach the Kennel Hill signpost at a junction. Go straight ahead, following 'North

Cream Teas, Tehidy Country Park

Cliff Car Park ¼ mile' (an underestimate!). At a meeting of several tracks, in a short distance, turn right for 100m, gently uphill. At a T-junction, with seat, bear right. Turn left at the next junction to return to the car park.

Walk 9: St Piran's Church and Oratory

Two very early Christian sites are situated at Penhale Sands, a huge area of dunes to the north of Perranporth. The church has surviving foundations and some minimal wall structure but the site of the Oratory, believed to have been abandoned as long ago as the 11th century, re-discovered in 1835 but since re-buried, is marked only by a granite stone on a mound. Close to the remains of the church is a tall granite cross.

Perranporth is a large holiday village of no particular distinction.

The out and back walk to the sites is entirely easy, on a good path. There are, however, several variations of this popular path, particularly near the start, where route finding needs care. There are no stiles or other impediments.

Distance	3¼ km (2 miles)
Ascent	40m (131ft)
Start/car parking	Adequate laybys at the side of a minor road, which leaves the B3285 a little more than one mile north east of Perranporth. The laybys are opposite a junction, grid reference 775553
Refreshments	None – drive to Perranporth
Map	Ordnance Survey Explorer 104, Redruth and St Agnes, 1:25,000

The Walk

Leave the layby through a kissing gate, with an information board on the right, to follow a well used track with a narrow, overgrown section which can be avoided by detouring to the left of the thickets. Nettle, bramble and gorse are all present. There is a diversity of paths across

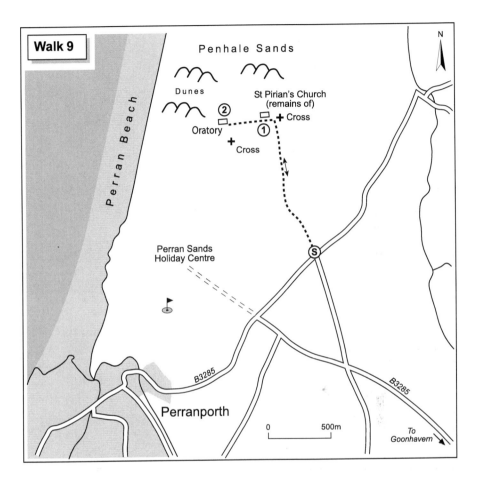

this rough land; keep to the waymarked posts and small white marker stones, heading just a little west of north.

The path becomes more certain; ignore a market post which points to a minor track on the left, soon reaching a tall granite cross at a junction of many paths. A few metres further is an information board and the excavated (250 tons of sand were removed!) remains of St Piran's Church.

1. Turn left to head west along a clear track, a little up and down, passing a waymarked post and a marker stone. Cross a bridge over

Remains of St Piran's Church

a gully and rise to the site of the Oratory, with information board and a large stone. The top of an adjacent dune has a wooden cross.

2. Return by the same route, turning right at the granite cross and heading towards Gear Farm.

Information Board, St Piran's Oratory

Walk 10: Godrevy Head and the Knavocks

A length of spectacular coast, including Godrevy Head and Navax Point, a few miles to the north-east of Hayle, is part of a major National Trust holding extending more than six miles. The land was acquired by the Trust primarily to prevent further seaward expansion of Cambourne and Redruth, holiday development of Gwithian and sand working south of Godrevy Towans.

The South West Coast Path crosses the area and there is extensive public access including beaches. 'Towans' are stabilised sand dunes; here they include Mesolithic archaeological sites preserved by wind-blown sand. The extensive earthwork running north-east, behind the toilet block, is probably 16th century. Near to the headland, at the highest point, is a pre-historic burial mound.

The area of the Knavocks is noted for its gorse, heather and 'open grassland' plant species. The views, particularly over St Ives Bay, are spectacular. Tracks are entirely good, with modest ascents at easy gradients; the short version has even less ascent.

Distance	6 km (3¾ miles) Short walk 2½ km (1½ miles)
Ascent	61m (200ft) Short walk 25m (82ft)
Start/car parking	National Trust Godrevy (lower) car park, grid reference 585422. Leave the B3301 half a mile north of Gwithian village
Refreshments	Godrevy Beach Café (seasonal) adjacent to the car park
Map	Ordnance Survey Explorer 102, Land's End, 1:25,000

The Walk

From the car park turn left, along the little road heading towards Godrevy Head, in a few metres diverting to the left to follow a sandy footpath which stays close to the road for most of the way to the upper car park. Pass a Lifeguard hut; there are already fine views to the left, across St Ives Bay. Godrevy Farm is to the right and the lighthouse on Godrevy Island is soon in view ahead. Join the road for a few metres then fork left along the waymarked South West Coast Path, directly towards the lighthouse. The upper car park and the

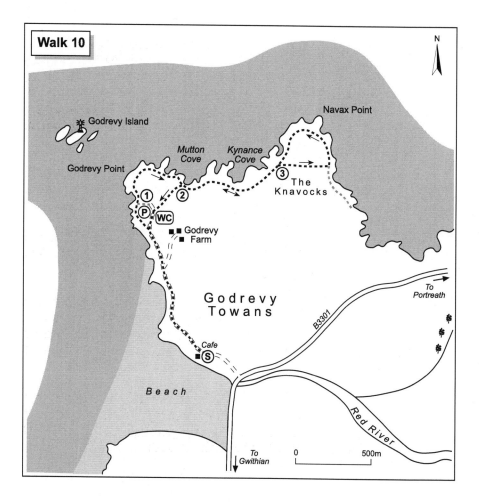

Beach near Godrevy Point

public conveniences (seasonal) are above to the right. Join the broad track which leads from the upper car park to the beach at a waymarked post. Turn right for 20m then bear left to a Cornish stile.

1. The path forks; keep right, rising, soon with views over the bay to the east, as far as St Agnes Beacon. Continue along the South West Coast Path.

2. Pass behind Mutton Cove, where a waymarked right turn gives a direct return to the upper car park for the short walk. Otherwise, continue along the well-worn path, still rising a little to pass behind Kynance Cove (not to be confused with its south coast and more spectacular namesake). Go through a kissing gate.

3. Bear right at a fork, now among the gorse and heather of the Knavocks. A trig point with National Trust sign marks the summit of this distinctive area. Go past the trig point to rejoin the coast path. Turn left to return to the fork, at point 3, and retrace the route to point 2.

Turn left here to descend to the upper car park and follow the access road past the public conveniences before forking right to rejoin the outward route, following the sandy path for most of the way back to the car park.

Coast Path, Godrevy Point

Walk 11: Lelant and St Ives

This walk largely uses the South West Coast Path through the extremely popular holiday area of Carbis Bay and St Ives, neither of which need much description. Suffice it to say that despite the crowds in high season St Ives is still a lovely little town with a good harbour, its many attractions enhanced in recent years by the construction of the Tate Gallery.

With a fair amount of rise and fall, including steps, the walk is rather harder than might be expected in such a civilised area. The return to Lelant Park and Ride is by train.

St Ives, Tate Gallery

Distance	7 km (4¼ miles)
Ascent	110m (361ft)
Start/car parking	Park and Ride car park adjacent to Lelant Saltings railway station, grid reference 543366
Refreshments	Hotels at Carbis Bay. Beach cafés at Porthminster Beach. Wide choice in St Ives
Map	Ordnance Survey Explorer 102, Land's End, Penzance and St Ives, 1:25,000

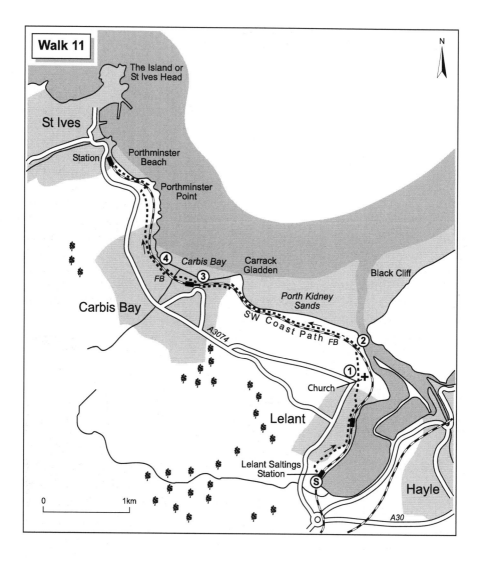

The Walk

From the payment hut at the entrance to the park and ride turn right, along a short footpath connecting to a minor road. Turn right to walk by the roadside along the very quiet road, part of the South West Coast Path. In about half a mile pass the tiny Lelant railway station and continue, gently uphill, towards Lelant church. Join a more important road, still rising gently towards the church.

1. By the entrance to the church, follow 'Coast Path, public footpath Carbis Bay 1¾ miles'. Go straight ahead at a waymarked cross paths. The path descends, with occasional steps, to cross a golf course, heading for a World War II blockhouse. Pass the blockhouse, keeping right to go under the railway.

2. Look carefully for a 'Coast Path' sign, turning left by the side of a house. The path rises between hedge banks, passing above the extensive Porth Kidney Sands. Pass the end of a footbridge over the railway, going straight ahead. The built-up area of Carbis Bay is in view. After a few steps down there is a steep ascent, with the aid of a handrail. Pass a railway crossing and go straight ahead at a junction in 20m. Cross the railway on a footbridge and continue, passing a house gate with a little plaque 'Chy-An-Kerries. Home of Barbara Hepworth and Ben Nicholson, 1943-1952'. Enter the Carbis Bay built-up area, turning right at a public road.

St Ives Harbour

3. Pass the entrance to Carbis Bay railway station and follow the road down to the Carbis Bay Hotel, passing below the front of the hotel along a broad track. After passing the hotel the track rises, with wide-spaced steps, to a footbridge over the railway. Cross and continue along a surfaced footpath, rising to a signpost 'Coast Path to St Ives', now an unsurfaced lane.

4. At a junction go straight ahead. There is a 'Coast Path' sign. The roadway becomes tarmac surfaced before the 'Baulking House' is reached, then descends to a fork. Go right, steeply downhill, at a 'Coast Path, public footpath, St Ives ½ mile' sign. There are seats, waymarks and a bridge over the railway before steps lead to the back of Porthminster Beach, with cafés, etc. Turn left to follow the roadway beside the railway, here on a low viaduct. Ascend a flight of steps on the left which leads directly into the car park of St Ives railway station.

Walk 12: Levant and Botallack

This part of North Cornwall is rich in the remains of the once great mining industry. The ruined engine houses, in particular, are now an iconic enhancement of the attractively rocky coast.

At Levant the National Trust has restored some of the buildings and the pumping engine operates on several days each week during the season. Mine workings extended for a considerable distance under the sea.

The remains of Botallack Mine are close to the neat little village of the same name, with the Queen's Arms Inn providing a good destination point for this out and back route.

This 'mini' walk provides a rare opportunity for 'level' walkers to enjoy the South West Coast Path, high above the sea, without significant rise or fall. The track is good underfoot, entirely easy, and there are numerous mining relics along the way.

Distance	4½km (2¾ miles)
Ascent	35m (115ft)
Start/car parking	Car park above the Levant Mine, grid reference 368345. Accessed along a minor road (Levant Road) leaving the B3306 at Trewellard (National Trust signpost)
Refreshments	Queen's Arms Inn at Botallack
Map	Ordnance Survey Explorer 102, Land's End, 1:25,000

Levant Mine

The Walk

Leave the car park along a broad track at the far (SW) end, part of the
South West Coast Path. Keep to the left of the overflow car park to
head towards a prominent building, 'Roscommon', up a long but
gentle rise. There are derelict mine buildings to right and left. Pass
'Roscommon', then above the remains of the well-known Botallack

Mine, the National Trust Counthouse Workshop and Botallack Manor before reaching the edge of Botallack village. Keep right at a junction to walk to the Queen's Arms Inn.

After suitable refreshment return to Levant by the same route, with Pendeen lighthouse in distant view.

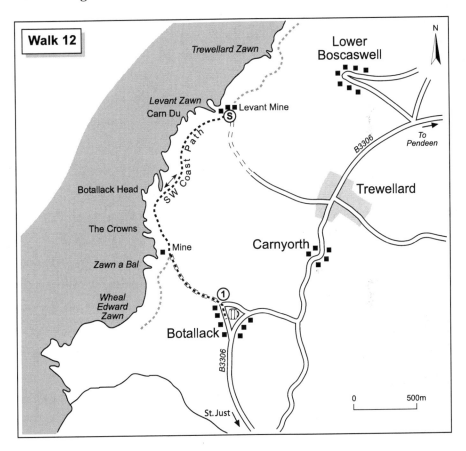

Walk 13: Sennen Cove and Land's End

Land's End really needs no introduction; for obvious reasons it continues to attract hordes of visitors. The granite cliff scenery is superb and has inspired rather fanciful names for some of the rock features. The Longships lighthouse guards the long line of jagged rocks which juts out to sea. On a clear day, the Scilly Isles, twenty-eight miles to the south west, are visible.

Superimposed on the natural attraction of this legendary place is a whole range of man-made edifices. The 'First and Last House' has long offered refreshments; much newer is a virtual shopping/ entertainment village, of necessity backed by extensive car parks. There is also a small Wildlife Discovery Centre.

Sennen Cove is an altogether different kind of place. Tucked in below the cliff at the south western end of the long beach of Whitesand Bay, there are still a few former fishermen's cottages and a jetty in what was formerly a remote hamlet.

Along the way, the rocky coast culminating in Land's End is unfailingly impressive and the various commercial attractions and refreshment opportunities may be of interest to many walkers.

Distance	6½km (4 miles)
Ascent	100m (328ft)
Start/car parking	Pay and Display car park on the Sennen Cove approach road, grid reference 359264. Turn right from the A30, 2½km (1½ miles) short of Land's End
Refreshments	Wide choice at Land's End
Map	Ordnance Survey Explorer 102, Land's End, 1:25,000

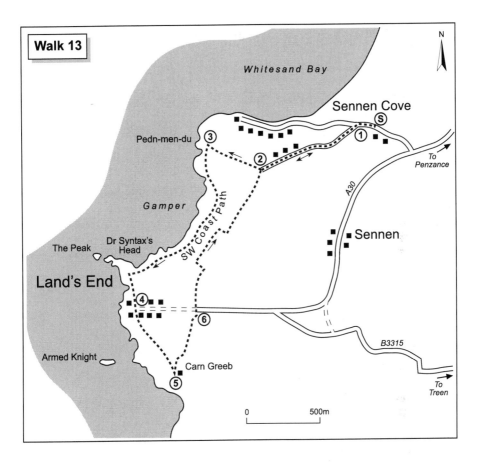

At Carn Greeb Farm is a craft centre and domestic animal farm.

Inevitably, the South West Coast Path provides the outward route for this superb short circular walk; the inland return is also excellent; there are no stiles and, apart from one section of narrow footpath, the tracks are broad and well-used. There are no steep or prolonged ascents.

The Walk

Turn right from the car park to walk along the roadside pavement downhill towards Sennen Cove for approximately 150m.

1. Turn left into a minor cul de sac road, Maria's Lane, initially with a footpath alongside. The lane rises at a gentle gradient, passing detached properties; there are fine views over Sennen Cove and Whitesand Bay and beach. The road bends to the left at a terrace of older cottages.

Land's End Sign

2. Turn right here to descend gently along a rough surfaced roadway, with great views of the beach.

3. As the roadway rakes back to the right, go left at a gate to follow the South West Coast Path towards Land's End (National Trust Mayon Cliff sign). A small deviation to the right reaches a castellated former coastguard lookout building of 1912. Continue towards Land's End along a generally broad track, with minor narrow rocky sections. The views continue to be superb

First and Last House, Land's End

as the track passes behind coves and headlands and there are carpets of thrift and other coastal flowers. Mini streams and the remains of old field boundaries add interest. Approaching the buildings at Land's End bear right to the low isolated 'First and Last House in England' building.

4. Continue to the main built-up area; public conveniences are included. Pass through the complex, then a small car park, to follow a good path heading for the visible buildings of Carn Greeb Farm. Just short of the farm join a tarmac roadway, continuing towards the farm.

5. After visiting the farm, return to the wishing well; in a further 10m fork right at a waymarked post (bridleway) to rise steeply for a very short distance A good but narrow path crosses an area of moorland vegetation – heather and gorse.

6. Reach the Land's End access road at a gate. Turn left, then right in 60m to go round an isolated property and join the Land's End exit road. Turn right for less than 50m then turn left to follow a fenced track, a bridleway, twisting and turning, with a good walking surface all the way back to point 2, close to the terrace of cottages. Ignore any footpaths which join the track. Retrace the outward route to the car park.

Sennen Cove

Walk 14: Sancreed and Carn Euny

Sancreed in a tiny village with a substantial granite church, two ancient crosses in the churchyard and a holy well. It is also the meeting place of several very minor roads.

The surrounding area is rich in its profusion of forts, standing stones and other bronze/iron age monuments. Paramount is the iron age village of Carn Euny, a remarkable settlement of courtyard houses probably built about 500 BC. Most intriguing is the 'fogou', believed to be of much earlier date, a semi-underground structure of dry stone walling, roofed with granite slabs. Despite appearances, this was not used as a burial chamber and its purpose remains a matter of conjecture. At least in Britain, 'fogous' are unique to Cornwall. Nearby is the hill fort of Caer Bran, its fortifications still visible.

Brane is a compact farming hamlet, close to Carn Euny.

The outward route is across a swathe of agricultural land, with paths not always clear on the ground, but easy enough to follow, from stile to stile. The return is generally along broad tracks but with one section which is narrow and somewhat overgrown. A half mile along a (quiet) road concludes the return to Sancreed. The aggregate ascent is above average.

Distance	5¾km (3½ miles)
Ascent	139m (456ft)
Start/car parking	Roadside layby a short distance beyond the residential area above the church in Sancreed, grid reference 419295
Refreshments	None en route
Map	Ordnance Survey Explorer 102, Land's End, 1:25,000

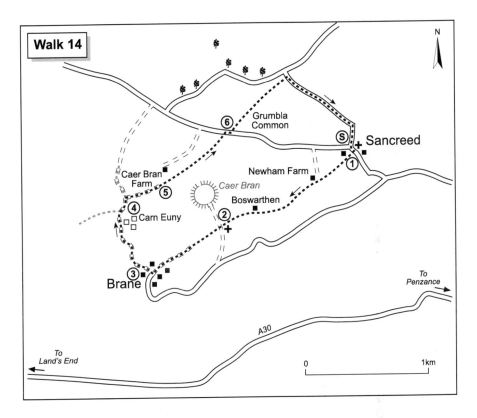

The Walk

Walk down the road towards the church in Sancreed village, passing a road junction.

1. Opposite the church gate turn right. The footpath is signposted, with a 'Holy Well' sign and a Cornish Ancient Sites Protection Network notice. Go up a few steps to follow the path between properties. The Holy Well may be visited by a fairly short, signposted, diversion to the right. Go over a stile, past a waymark on a post. Keep close to the field boundary on the right to reach another stile in the corner. Pass Newham Farm, bearing right to yet another stile and keeping a fairly straight line across the next field to head for a property in a shallow valley. Pass to the right of the property, go straight ahead at a post with multiple waymarks and

Boswarthen Farm, Sancreed

keep to the right of a second property. After another stile the path rises steadily along the right hand boundary of a field. After more stiles an abandoned farm, 'Boswarthen', is reached. Pass to the left of the buildings, still rising as more fields are crossed.

2. Reach an unsurfaced lane at a waymarked gate/stile. Cross the lane to a stile by an ancient cross. There are more gates and stiles as the path goes gently downhill towards Brane hamlet. A little lane leads into the hamlet. Go between the buildings to a road junction.

3. Turn right; there is a 'Carn Euny' signpost. At a small car park the track forks; go to the right (signposted 'Carn Euny') to rise gently between high hedge banks to a gate/stile. Continue along a narrow field, soon bearing left through a gateway to reach a kissing gate giving access to the site.

4. Start the return by leaving Carn Euny at the side opposite to the entrance; a not very obvious narrow path and down a few steps. Pass a house and turn right at a junction in a few metres.

5. In less than 200m turn right, opposite farm gates to head in a north-easterly direction; Caer Bran Farm is prominent to the left,

ahead. The track soon becomes a footpath with narrow and overgrown sections. Continue, soon joining an unsurfaced roadway, now close to Caer Bran Farm. Go left to follow this roadway, a fine walking route leading to the St Just to Sancreed road; the iron age fort is to the right of the route and there are extensive views.

6. Turn right at the road then, in a few metres, turn left through a gate to take a signposted bridleway along the edge of Grumbla Common. Keep away from the remains of old mining workings. Go right at a fork and straight ahead at the next fork to head towards dwellings in the valley bottom. There are impressive bluebells in Spring. Go through a little gate and continue, soon joining a public highway at a group of buildings.

Turn right to walk by the roadside, initially uphill, passing the Sancreed boundary sign before reaching the parking layby.

Carn Euny

Walk 15: Penzance, Newlyn and Mousehole

As the principal town of West Cornwall and the terminus of the main railway line from Paddington, Penzance is an attractively bustling place with all the expected facilities. It is also a considerable port, with two harbours.

Mousehole is very different, a traditional fishing port with curving stone quays backed by a village with narrow, picturesque streets. Even in high season, when crowded, much of the charm is still apparent. Occupying much of the coastline between the two, Newlyn is a mixture of old fishing port, reputedly the busiest in Cornwall, and sprawling residential area. Late in the 19th century Newlyn became the focal point of an important movement in English art – the 'Newlyn School' – of which Stanhope Forbes was the 'father'. In more recent times St Ives has assumed greater importance as a West Country centre of the arts.

This linear walk is unlike any other in the book, using a length of the South West Coast Path which is largely urbanised, but is never without interest for the walker, with ports, beaches, long views to Mounts Bay and St Michael's Mount and always the sea. Underfoot the mixture of

Distance	6 km (3¾ miles)
Ascent	25m (82ft)
Start/car parking	Huge pay and display car park close to the railway station in Penzance, grid reference 477305
Refreshments	Inns and cafés at Newlyn, Mousehole and Penzance
Map	Ordnance Survey Explorer 102, Land's End, 1:25,000

Mousehole Harbour

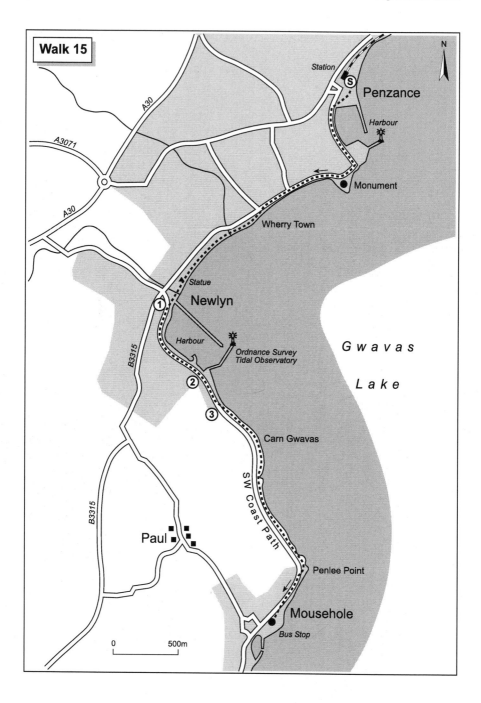

Walk 15

Penzance

Station

S

Harbour

Monument

A30

A3071

A30

Wherry Town

Statue

① Newlyn

Harbour

Ordnance Survey
Tidal Observatory

②

③

B3315

Carn Gwavas

G w a v a s

L a k e

SW Coast Path

B3315

Paul

Penlee Point

Mousehole

Bus Stop

0   500m

N

hard tracks and roadside pavement makes the wearing of boots unnecessary. The return is by the half hourly bus service from the harbour at Mousehole back to the main car park in Penzance.

The Walk

Head for the vehicular entrance/exit to the car park. Turn left to walk by the roadside, crossing the swing bridge, with an inner harbour to the right and a commercial harbour on the left. Penzance parish church is prominent on the hill ahead. Pass the Dolphin Tavern, then a monument and a large public swimming pool on the left, continuing along the promenade towards Newlyn, visible across the sweep of its wide bay. After passing public conveniences the walkway becomes more separated from the road, with a small park including children's

Newlyn Harbour

play area and a bowling green. After an interesting Fishermen's monument, the Tolcarne Inn and some attractive cottages, the centre of Newlyn is reached over a bridge.

1. Cross the main road and turn left. To the right is Duke Street Café. Pass old inns – the Swordfish and the Dolphin. To the left are the extensive docks, with fish landing/auction sheds. Continue uphill past the Red Lion and public conveniences, soon reaching the start of a signposted cycle/walkway descending gently towards the sea.

2. Follow this excellent hard surfaced track until it rises to rejoin the road. Walk along the generous roadside pavement for less than 200m, looking carefully for a waymarked gap in the roadside fence.

3. Turn left here, descending steps, then a narrow path, before reaching a concrete walkway along the top of the sea wall. This walkway provides a fine level route round the end

Fisherman Statue, Newlyn

of Penlee Point all the way to Mousehole, passing below the old Penlee Lifeboat Station. The Penlee lifeboat was involved in a sea disaster in 1981, when all the lifeboat crew perished. The track rises into a car park. Go through the car park to reach the harbour. The bus terminus is towards the far end.

Walk 16: Helston and Porthleven

A pleasant small town, with curving streets and steep alleys, the ancient borough of Helston is most famous for its traditional floral or 'furry' dance. Below the town is an extensive public recreation area with a boating lake and other attractions.

Porthleven, just a few miles from Helston, is a delightful fishing and leisure port with inner and outer harbours. The parish church of St Bartholomew, built in 1842, is at the sea end of the harbour. More prominent inland is a Wesleyan Chapel, built in 1890.

Loe Pool is the largest freshwater lake in Cornwall, brought about by the natural formation of Loe Bar. By the 13th century, the estuary of the River Cober gradually became dammed by the build up of silt residues, washed down from the numerous tin and copper mines in the area, forming a continuous barrier across the mouth. For many years a channel was periodically dug through the Bar in order to alleviate flooding higher up the estuary. The Pool has become a great centre for wildlife. The adjacent land is within the historic Penrose Estate, with an extended 17th century manor house: the estate was gifted to the National Trust in 1974.

Distance	7 km (4¼ miles)
Ascent	45m (148ft)
Start/car parking	Huge free car park 'Fairground' by the side of the road from Helston to Porthleven, B3304, half a mile south-west of Helston town centre, grid reference 653270
Refreshments	Two inns, cafés (and a Cornish pasty shop) in Porthleven
Map	Ordnance Survey Explorer 103, The Lizard, 1:25,000

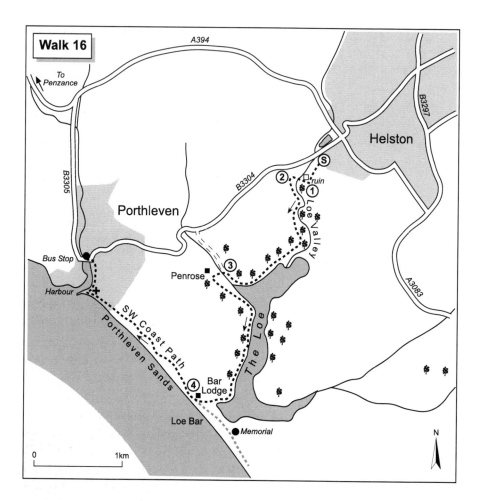

The walk is entirely easy, on good tracks, largely beside Loe Pool, then following part of the South West Coast Path into Porthleven, with the return to Helston using the frequent bus service.

The Walk

Go to the far end of the car park to find a track to the left of a 'Penrose Amenity Area' sign, joining a concrete roadway in a few metres. Turn right, to follow this roadway through mixed woodland. In approximately half a mile pass the remains of a chimney which once served a silver mine.

1. In a further 50m look carefully for a minor path on the right. Turn right to descend rudimentary steps and cross the shallow valley of the River Coble. The wet ground of Loe Marsh, with suitably lush vegetation, rich in alder and willow, is crossed by a good path. Cross the river on a bridge and join a broad unsurfaced roadway.

2. Turn left to follow the roadway through the fine mature woodland of Oak Grove, passing a small tunnel on the right. There are occasional seats and glimpses of Loe Pool. At Helston Lodge, a trim Victorian property with great views, go through a little gate and across the front of the house. Continue along a tarmac road, soon with Penrose House in view ahead.

3. Turn left at a road junction to rise gently past the stable block of Penrose House. As the road bears to the right, go straight ahead along a track signposted 'Porthleven. Loe Bar via coastal route'. The

Helston

Porthleven

track loses its hard surface as it rises gently, with views over the water. There are more seats and the various parts of a National Trust 'Green Gymnasium' of various exercise equipment. The track crosses a hillside, terraced above the water; there is a long, gentle, rise as the sea and the Loe Bar sandbank come into view. At the far end of the Bar the Anson Memorial, marking the loss of the frigate 'Anson' just off the Bar in 1807, with the drowning of more than 100 members of the crew, is visible.

4. Reach the detached house, Bar Lodge, with an information board adjacent. Go through a small gate; the South West Coast Path joins from the left and Porthleven is soon in view. The path is somewhat up and down; after a rise descend steps and a steep little path to a small car park with a 'Coast Path. Porthleven Harbour ½ mile' sign. An unsurfaced roadway goes steadily uphill to reach the fringe of Porthleven. Join a more important road to descend towards the church and harbour. Pass the church to walk along the side of the outer and inner harbours, with cafés, inn and pasty shop. Turn left to reach the obvious bus stop behind the inner harbour.

Walk 17: Lizard Point

Britain's most southerly point, the Lizard, is famous for its part in the history of radio communications and for its lighthouse, the first structure (short-lived) dating from 1619. There is a visitor centre (open only during summer) at the present lighthouse. The first radio signal was sent to Newfoundland by Marconi in 1901.

The cliff scenery is spectacular, including olive green serpentine and with the tops bedecked with colourful flowers.

Lizard village is situated around a large green used for car parking, not particularly attractive, very open and often windswept. There are shops, cafés and an inn. Serpentine, fashioned into ornaments of many shapes and sizes, is a popular favourite in the local gift shops.

Distance	4km (2½ miles)
Ascent	100m (328ft)
Start/car parking	National Trust car park, with public conveniences, close to Lizard Point, grid reference 702116
Refreshments	Cafés at Lizard Point. Inn and cafés in Lizard village
Map	Ordnance Survey Explorer 103, The Lizard, Falmouth and Helston, 1:25,000

The Walk

Start by crossing the car park exit road, heading towards the sea, passing an information board. Follow 'Lizard Point via steps and path', soon reaching a T-junction with marvellous coastal views. Choose between the steps and the path to descend to the motley buildings and a little car park at the Point. Bear right to rise along the access road for a few metres.

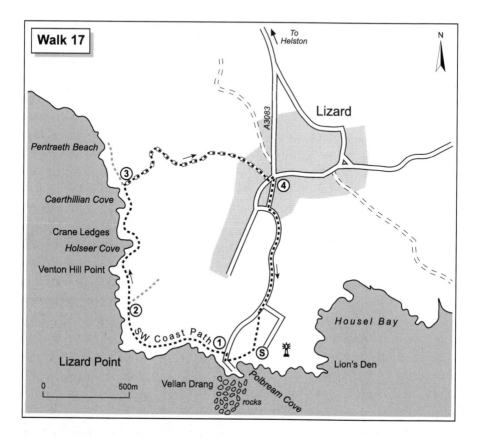

1. At a sign 'Coast Path. Public footpath. Kynance Cove 2½ miles' turn
left, across the front of a café. Pass a National Trust 'Pistil Meadow'
sign and descend steps before crossing a little bridge. Go up rough
steps at the start of the second longest ascent of the route, over the
headland of Lizard Point, never really steep and good underfoot.
The coast path is now basically level for some distance, above the
impressive sea cliffs and with an old stone wall on the right. Pass
a National Nature Reserve (Caerthillian) information board. The
area is particularly rich in wild flowers.

2. A right fork leading to Lizard village is passed; unless a speedy
return is desired, ignore this. Descend to Holseer Cove, cross a tiny
stream and rise a few metres to continue to Caerthillian Cove,
descending again to cross two adjacent streams.

3. A few metres after crossing the streams turn right (there is a path 10m after the first stream; ignore this). The main ascent of the route now climbs steadily but not steeply inland, initially on the side of a valley. Join an unmade roadway close to a house. Follow the roadway to the centre of Lizard village, with its large green used as a car park, with public conveniences.

4. Follow 'most southerly point' at a signpost, going left then right to leave the village along the road to Lizard Point, passing the Witch Ball, claimed to be a 15th century inn. Take a roadside footpath signposted 'National Trust. Lizard Point', which avoids use of the road for some distance. There are seats along the way. The lighthouse comes into view. As the path rejoins the road go straight across to a similar footpath which leads directly into the National Trust car park.

At Lizard Point

Walk 18: Helford and Frenchman's Creek

With one of the best known names in Cornwall, the charming village of Helford, formerly the haunt of pirates and smugglers, is now a leisure boating paradise, clustered beautifully around an inlet from the main Helford River. Facilities include a post office/stores, café and inn. Thanks to Daphne du Maurier, Frenchman's Creek has an equally iconic name. In truth that creek, apart from the literary references, is neither more nor less interesting than others around the estuary. It is a pleasant waterway with heavily wooded banks.

A short distance inland, Manaccan is a village of quiet charm with inn and shop; the parish church of St Manacca has a Norman south door. Because the spine of high ground separating Helford and Frenchman's Creek must be crossed twice, this walk has more than the usual amount of ascent. Omitting Frenchman's Creek, as suggested in point 2 below, results in a shorter, less demanding, route. The mixture of footpaths, broader tracks and some minor road includes several Cornish stiles.

Distance	9km (5½ miles)
Ascent	162m (532ft)
Start/car parking	Large pay and display car park at Helford village, grid reference 759261. Helford is reached only by minor roads, via Gweek, St Martin and Newtown St Martin from the Falmouth/Truro direction
Refreshments	Inns at Helford and Manaccan, Riverside Café at Helford
Map	Ordnance Survey Explorer 103, The Lizard, 1:25,000

Helford

The Walk

From the car park turn right to descend the road into Helford village. Cross the creek on the footbridge by the ford. Turn right to walk along the road, passing the Post Office/stores and the inn. Stay with the road as it bends to the left, sharply uphill. In less than 100m, after the bend, turn right at a 'public footpath' sign to follow a well-used path. Pass a gate and waymarks on posts. Descend past a National Trust sign 'footpath to Penarvon Cove'. A wooded path above the water leads to Penarvon Cove.

1. At a 'Frenchman's Creek' sign bear left to commence the long ascent of a roadway, part tarmac surfaced. Go straight ahead at a junction.

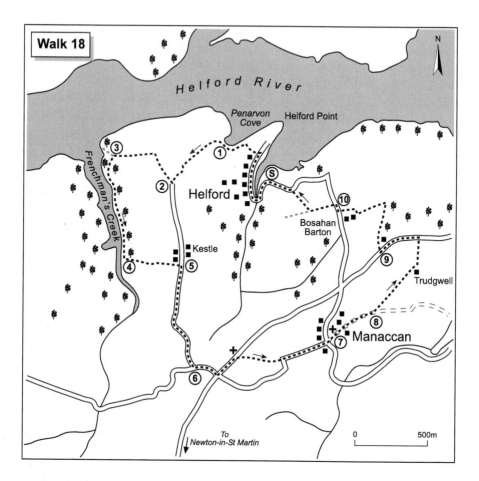

2. At a T-junction with 'Frenchman's Creek. Permissive Path' signpost turn right, along a broad, unsurfaced, roadway (a left turn here omits the Frenchman's Creek section of the route, saving some distance and approximately 66m (217ft) of ascent). At a fork on a bend go left along a lesser track, downhill through cultivated farming land.

3. Close to the bottom, turn left through a kissing gate and down steps, with National Trust 'Frenchman's Creek, permissive footpath' sign. A clear path winds its way along the side of the

lushly vegetated creek, up and down a little. Pass a seat with a view and ignore a path with steps on the right.

4. After about three quarters of a mile the path bears to the left for the second long ascent, a quite steep rough roadway.. At the top keep to the left edge of a field and pass the large 'Kestle' farmstead.

5. Joint the public road at a gate. Turn right to walk by the side of a very quiet road. Turn left at a junction, signposted to 'Helford'.

6. At the next junction go left, again signposted to 'Helford' to head for a substantial Methodist chapel. Eighty metres before the chapel turn right, over a stile with a 'public footpath' sign. Cross a meadow to another stile, then a second meadow to a third stile. Keep to the

Helford River

right edge of a third meadow to yet another stile and join a surfaced lane by the Manaccan boundary sign. Go straight ahead to reach the village.

7. Cross the main village road to a narrow path opposite. Join a minor road by the village shop, rising to a junction; the church is to the left. Go right at a junction with a 'cul de sac. public bridleway' sign. Rise very gently, initially passing detached houses. The road loses its hard surface, becoming a pleasant lane across farming land.

8. In approximately 400m go left at a fork with a 'public footpath' sign. Go over an easy stile and continue through 'Trudgwell' farmstead. Follow the farm access road to join a minor public road. Turn left to walk by the roadside for 300m, passing a thatched house, part of the Bosahan Estate.

9. One hundred metres past the house turn right, along a signposted path, with long views over farming land, passing through two old kissing gates. Turn left at a 'Helford' sign opposite the second gate. Approaching a large farming complex, 'Bosahan Barton', turn right to follow the route signposted along the near edge of a huge field. After turning right at the corner, leave the field over a low stile on the left to join a road. Turn right, downhill.

10. Turn left in a few metres, along a roadway to a picnic and viewing area. Continue for less than 200m. The views over the Helford River are extensive. Turn right at a 'public footpath' sign to descend steadily along the left edge of a field. As the path narrows keep close to the hedge bank on the left, soon joining the Helford access road, turning left to descend to the car park.

Walk 19: Argol and College Reservoirs

The reservoirs are both attractive sheets of water, close to Falmouth yet undeniably off the beaten track. Routes can be linked to make one walk or separated into two walks, of equal length but of different character.

Argol has more open countryside and a good path throughout with no stiles and just a few gates.

College is more heavily wooded with extensive areas of marsh and appropriate vegetation. The path is aided by lengths of boardwalk, some of which are in poor condition, and there is overgrown and boggy ground.

Distance	Full walk 7km (4¼ miles)
Ascent	Full walk 65m (213ft) Argol 30m (98ft) College 35m (115ft)
Start/car parking	Pay and display car park with picnic area, public conveniences and children's play area near the foot of Argol Reservoir, grid reference 762328
Refreshments	Picnic only
Map	Ordnance Survey Explorer 105, Falmouth and Mevagissey, 1:25,000

The Walk

Start at a signpost 'Round Reservoir Walk' at the far end of the car park, along a clear path, initially gravelled. The route is always clear on the ground, with woodland and open sections alternating. There are occasional seats and Mabe Church is prominent on the hillside

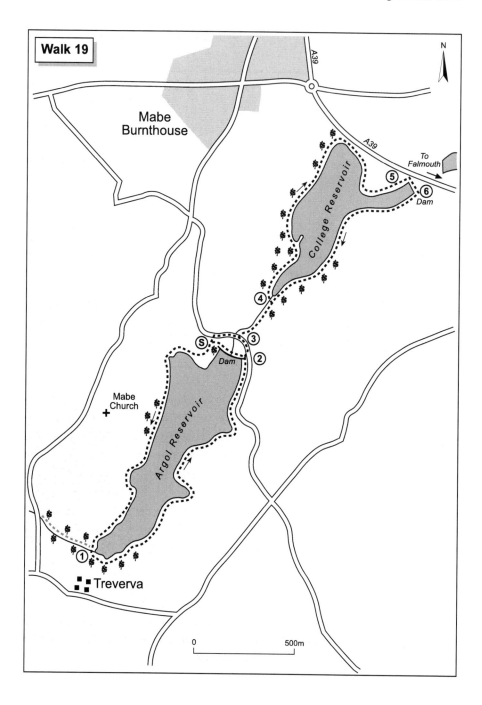

above as is Treverva village on high ground at the head of the reservoir.

1. Close to the far end of the reservoir keep left at a junction, soon entering a nature reserve and passing a bird-watching hide, Campion, foxgloves, cow parsley and a variety of trees all contribute to the attraction of this area. Continue along the side of the water; the best view of the church is from this section of the path as it rises and falls gently. The dam at the foot of the reservoir comes into view. Pass below a house.

2. Go through a small gate on the left to walk along the top of the dam (well protected). Go through a gate at the far end and pass more seats before ascending steps. Pass a signpost and a stone building with fishery notice, bearing right through a gate, then left into the car park.

Those intending to do the full walk should not go through the gate at 2 above, but should continue ahead to join the public road. Turn left, downhill and look carefully for point 3 on the right.

Argol Reservoir

For the College Reservoir walk leave the car park by the vehicular access. Turn right to walk downhill by the roadside for nearly 200m

3. Turn left at a very small gap in the roadside foliage as the road bends, almost opposite a locked gate. The path is well established but is narrow and, in part, overgrown.

4. Keep left at a fork, soon crossing a little bridge. There are long lengths of boardwalk over marshy ground, through quite dense woodland. Cross another bridge; the path now clings close to the water and, at the reservoir foot, is also close to the main A39 road. There are more overgrown sections and some decrepit boardwalk, with just a few good waterside viewpoints.

5. Go up stone steps, cross a little bridge and descend, to left then right, to reach steps giving access to the dam. Walk across behind the dam and pass between boulders to reach a broad track at a waymarked post.

6. Turn right to rise a little past fine rhododendrons. The track soon becomes a narrow path, close to the water. The way is never in doubt but there are more decrepit boardwalks and some serious mud before the junction at point 4 is reached. Retrace from here to point 3 and turn right for a steady roadside ascent back to the car park.

Walk 20: Flushing and Mylor Churchtown

Facing Falmouth across the estuarial Penryn River, Flushing is a quietly attractive little place with inns and café and some of the buildings having a distinctly Dutch appearance.

On the far side of the headland, Mylor has a long maritime tradition. In the days when Falmouth was a packet boat port, much servicing of the boats was carried out at Mylor. The quays and boatyards at Mylor Churchtown now support an active leisure sailing industry. A little way inland, the parish church of St Mylor has a detached bell tower. In the churchyard is the Ganges Memorial, erected in 1872, commemorating the deaths of 53 young boys on the naval training ship HMS Ganges, moored at Mylor from 1866 to 1899.

This circular route links Mylor and Flushing, using one of the easiest sections of the coast path. Much of the inland return route is along a delightful wooded valley. The only significant ascent is the first part of the return route from Flushing, quite prolonged but not too steep. From the coast path the views across the water to Falmouth and the docks are splendid.

Distance	7 km (4¼ miles)
Ascent	80m (263ft)
Start/car parking	Substantial pay and display car parks, with public conveniences, in the boatyard area of Mylor Churchtown, grid reference 821353
Refreshments	Two inns and a café at Flushing. Castaways Bar and Café at Mylor Churchtown
Map	Survey Explorer 105, Falmouth and Mevagissey (or Explorer 103, The Lizard), 1:25,000

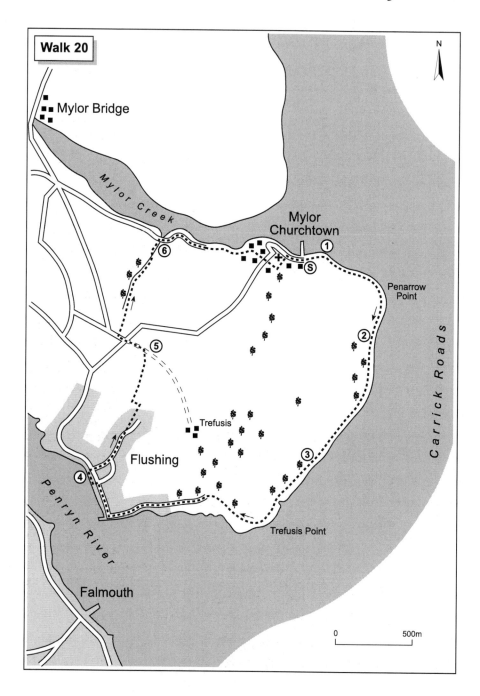

Walk 20

Mylor Bridge

Mylor Creek

Mylor Churchtown

Penarrow Point

Carrick Roads

Trefusis

Flushing

Penryn River

Falmouth

Trefusis Point

N

0   500m

The Walk

From the parking area walk back to the quayside road. There is a multi signpost.

1. Turn right towards 'Castaways Bar and the Seafood Restaurant'. Pass a 'public footpath to Flushing' sign. The broad, easy, track soon loses its surface. In about 100m, by the entrance to Penharrow House, the track bears to the right. Fork left here, along a narrow path, soon passing the Restronguet Sailing Club.

2. Go over a stile to enter the Trefusis Estate. The track is easy to follow, along the bottom edge of a field, with views across the estuary and with hedgerows of honeysuckle and wild briar, passing behind Penarrow Point. Pendennis Castle comes into view, followed by Falmouth Docks. Pass below a belt of woodland, go over a stile, cross a little stream and continue around the low headland.

3. At a gate, with granite grid stile beside, enter woodland. Reach a surfaced lane, go right through a gap beside a gate, and continue along a public road. Where the road descends to the left towards the estuary, fork right to rise up a surfaced track with a 'public footpath' sign. Go through a gate at the top to a public recreation area, the 'Bowling Green', with great views of Falmouth and numerous seats. Pass a children's play area and public conveniences, then descend along a surfaced path, soon joining a tarmac road. Turn left, join another road in 40m, reaching the estuary-side road at the Seven Stars Inn.

4. Turn right. At the next road junction, by the Royal Standard Inn, turn right to commence the most demanding ascent of the route. As the road bends to the right, becoming Orchard Vale, look carefully for steps on the left, with a 'public footpath Mylor Church 1 mile' signpost. After ascending the (few) steps, continue along a narrow but clear path. Go over a stile and along the edge of a huge cultivated field, the path now rising very gently. Go left over a waymarked stile just before a detached house.

5. Bear right before turning left along an access roadway. Go straight across a public road to follow another public road, signposted to

Mylor Bridge; turn right in 60m at a 'public footpath Trelew' sign.
Go down three granite steps to follow a descending path, soon
entering woodland. Keep right at a fork, still descending, the path
now a little rough underfoot, through attractively varied woodland.
Go through a gate and continue ahead, ignoring any paths to left or
right. Cross over a tiny stream before joining a lane. Turn right, as
indicated by a waymark.

6. Join a surfaced lane by Trelew. Turn right, downhill. There is soon
   a view of Mylor Creek on the left. There is a sharp little rise, then
   an elevated roadside footpath for some distance. As the road loses
   its surface, keep left at a 'footpath only' sign. There is another
   short rise before the public road to Mylor Churchtown is reached.
   Go straight across to descend past Mylor Church, with the 'HMS
   Ganges' memorial and a tall Celtic cross in the churchyard. Go
   through a gate at the bottom to reach the quayside road. Turn right
   to reach the car parking area in 50m.

Ferry to Falmouth

Walk 21: Idless Wood

Just a few miles to the north of Truro is a fine and well varied expanse of woodland, with various names for different parts – Lord's Wood, Lady's Wood, St Clement Woods, Bishop's Wood – all referring to historic ownership. As the hamlet of Idless is close by, with its name used by the Forestry Commission, it is appropriate to use 'Idless' for the whole area. Beech, oak, hazel, birch, holly, willow and Japanese larch are all present, with plentiful wild flowers, including bluebells, particularly on the outward route, where a stream accompanies the path for most of the way.

In previous centuries this was very much a working woodland with charcoal burning, basket making and other woodland industries. There is still evidence of the tree coppicing which was an essential part of these various activities.

At the highest point of the forest an iron age fort/settlement, its defensive embankments heavily overgrown, can be visited by making a short detour.

Distance	5½km (3½ miles)
Ascent	50m (164ft)
Start/car parking	Forestry Commission car park less than half a mile north of Idless hamlet, grid reference 821478. From Truro head north-west along the road towards Perranporth, B3284. Turn right at a sign for 'Idless' approximately a quarter mile after passing under a railway bridge
Refreshments	None en route
Map	Ordnance Survey Explorer 105, Falmouth and Mevagissey, 1:25,000

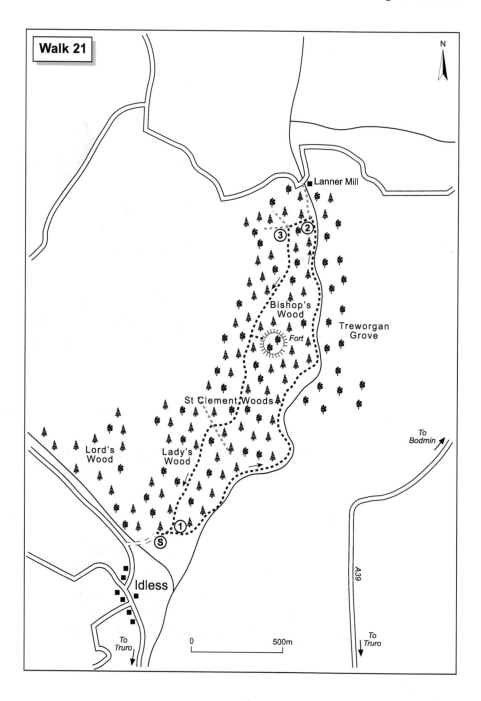

Walk 21

N

Lanner Mill

③ ②

Bishop's
Wood

Treworgan
Grove

Fort

St Clement Woods

Lord's
Wood

Lady's
Wood

To
Bodmin

①

Ⓢ

A39

Idless

To
Truro

0   500m

To
Truro

The circular route of this walk, all on good, easy, tracks, allows a full appreciation of the woodland, apparently used more by local residents than by holidaymakers. The only significant ascent is a fairly steep 30m (98ft) at the turning point of the walk.

The Walk

Pass the vehicular barrier at the far end of the car park to take a broad forestry roadway.

1. At a major fork keep right, soon with a stream below to the right. The track stays close to the bottom edge of the woodland, with the stream gurgling close by. Ignore several tracks on the left. There are occasional seats by the wayside and an abundance of bramble. Stay with the main track as it narrows, keeping right at a fork.

Idless Wood Sign

2. At a main junction, in approximately one and a half miles from the start, turn left uphill.

   If you miss this turn, you reach a vehicular barrier and a minor road in a further 100m. The former Lanner Mill is a short distance down this road to the right.

   The ascent is steady, on a good track.

3. At a cross tracks turn left, still rising for a short distance. The track soon becomes a forest roadway. Pass a vehicle turning circle; the iron age fort can be seen to the left in a further half mile. A short diversion along a minor path is required to visit the fort. Return to the main roadway and continue, ignoring waymarked paths to right and left. The roadway descends gently to the fork at point 1 for the return to the car park.

Walk 22: St Just in Roseland and St Mawes

Roseland (heath not roses!) is the substantial peninsula facing Falmouth across Carrick Roads, the estuary of the River Fal. St Just is a modest village with a highly esteemed church sited on a hillside, with the churchyard falling steeply from the lych gate, almost to estuary level, and the church itself nestling at the bottom. Flanked by banks of flowering shrubs the ornate tombstones cascade down the hillside.

St Mawes is a pleasant and dignified holiday resort with a fine situation at the tip of the peninsula. In order to guard the entrance to Carrick Roads, in about 1540 King Henry VIII built forts here and at Pendennis across the water. The older part of the town was then close to the fort. The town was granted Borough status in 1562, sending two members to Parliament; there are some cottages from these early times below the church. A nineteenth century harbour was destroyed by gales. Modern facilities include inns, cafés, shops and tourist information.

This circuit includes a very easy part of the South-West Coast Path along the side of the estuary, a walk along the sea front at St Mawes and a rather more difficult series of tracks ascending across agricultural land on the east side of the peninsula

Distance	9½km (6 miles), with easier options
Ascent	100m (328ft)
1 HR Start/car parking	Small car park immediately above the churchyard at St Just in Roseland, grid reference 849357 TR2 5JD
Refreshments	Choice of inns and cafés in St Mawes
Map	Ordnance Survey Explorer 105, Falmouth and Mevagissey, 1:25,000

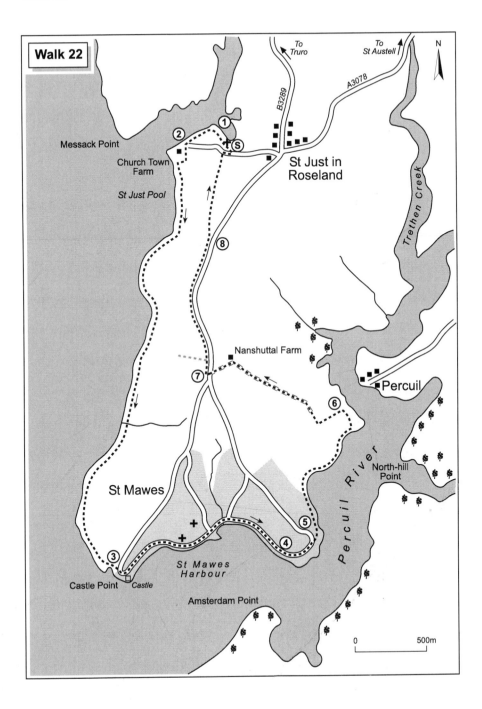

The Walk

Start by walking down through the celebrated churchyard.

1. Pass the church then bear left along a good path by the side of the creek. Go through a little gate before bearing right to pass close to boat sheds. There is a 'public footpath to St Mawes 2 miles' sign. Continue along a tarmac private road for about 100m.

2. Turn left through a small gate with a 'National Trust. Churchtown Farm' sign. The path ahead is now clear, predominantly over grass, all the way to St Mawes. Ignore any gates on the right which lead to the estuary foreshore. There are several (easy) stiles, gates and a bridge over a little stream. The views across the estuary to Mylor Churchtown, Falmouth and Pendennis Castle are superb.

3. Reach a large house on the left and the end of a surfaced road at the fringe of St Mawes. The road rises a little, heading for St Mawes Castle. Just before the castle a footpath forks to the right, saving a little ascent before rejoining the road and continuing to the centre of St Mawes, with shops, refreshments, public conveniences and Tourist Information Centre. The easy options are now either to return to St Just by the same route or to return by bus (number 50 at two hourly intervals).

Historic AA Sign, St Mawes

4. For the full walk continue along the road as it bends to the left behind Polvarth Point.

5. Turn right at Polvarth Lane, heading downhill to a creek-side boatyard. Before the boatyard turn left, up a few steps to follow 'public footpath Porthcuel Creek'. At another boatyard roadway turn right for a few metres, then left. Pass an isolated property then go over a waymarked stile, along a rather overgrown path, before

rising gently across a meadow. Bear left at a fork to head for a waymarked post.

6. At a post with several waymarks bear (not turn) left, uphill. Go through a gate and continue to rise across a meadow. On approaching a gate (do not go through) turn right (waymark) and keep the hedge on the left, soon reaching another gate, followed by a rough lane. Go straight ahead at a junction , the path now narrow and somewhat overgrown. The path leads to a more open lane, with long views. Go through several gates at Nanshuttel Farm. Ignore the waymark on the right and follow the farm access drive to join the main road, A3078, close to a prominent water tower.

7. Turn right, along the roadside, for 50m then turn left at a lane. Immediately on the right is a stile with a 'National Trust. Tregear Vean' sign. Go over and continue over grass along a fine route provided for walkers to avoid the potentially busy road. With the

Granite cross, St Just in Roseland

extra elevation, the views towards Falmouth are finer even than on the outward part of the route.

8. Go over a stile to join a lane. Turn left along the lane 'footpath to St Just. ½ mile'. The lane becomes a narrower path passing across the front of Church Farm Mill before descending steps to join the road a short distance below the car park. Turn right to return.

Walk 23: Dodman Point

Although not far from the popular resorts of Gorrans Haven and Mevagissey, Dodman Point stands high and lonely at the eastern end of Veryan Bay. It is a fine viewpoint, decorated with a large granite cross provided by the Rector of nearby St Michael Caerhays in 1896. The diligent may also find a late 18th century watch hut, restored by the National Trust. Much of the headland was included in an iron age fort, evidenced by the mighty 'bulwark' on the route of this walk. Local folklore has the name of the Point as 'Deadman', possibly referring to shipwrecks on the unforgiving rocks below.

The route uses a comparatively level section of the South West Coast Path, with an inland return which is largely along a very minor road, with splendid views. There are no problems underfoot; just three stiles if the short cut is taken at the end.

Dexter cattle grazing near Dobman Point

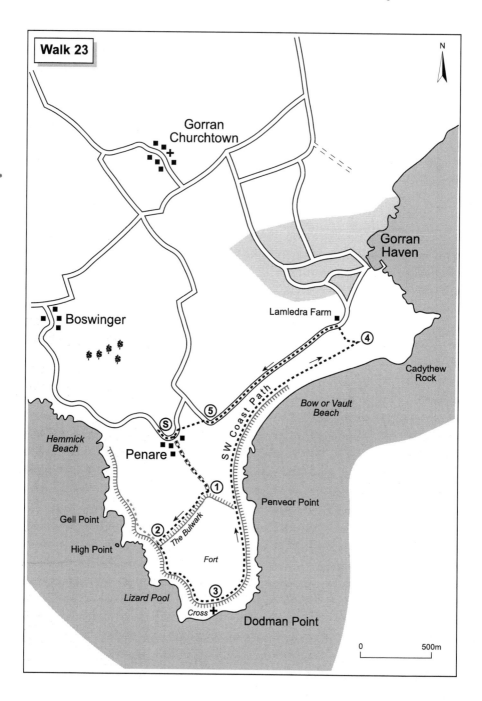

Walk 23

N

Gorran
Churchtown

Gorran
Haven

Lamledra Farm

Boswinger

④

Cadythew
Rock

⑤

Bow or Vault
Beach

Ⓢ

Hemmick
Beach

Penare

SW Coast Path

Gell Point

①

Penveor Point

②

The Bulwark

High Point

Fort

Lizard Pool

③

Cross

Dodman Point

0   500m

Distance	6½ km (4 miles)
Ascent	Negligible
Start/car parking	National Trust car park at Penare, approximately one and a half miles south west of Gorran Haven, reached by very minor roads from the A390 Truro to St Austell road, grid reference 000404
Refreshments	None en route. Inn and café at Gorran Haven
Map	Ordnance Survey Explorer 105, Falmouth and Mevagissey, 1:25,000

The Walk

Leave the car park by the vehicular entrance/exit, beside an information board. Go straight ahead, along the road, with Lower Penare Farmhouse on the left. As the road bends to the left go straight ahead along a broad unsurfaced roadway signposted 'Dodman Point and link to Coast Path', rising a little past a gate. The sea is in view both to left and right through gateways.

1. At the next gate stay with the track as it bears right, soon beside the 'Bulwark', a remarkable defensive rampart with high hedge banks. A track to the left leads up to the 'fort'. Continue to a signposted gate.

2. Turn left, along the Coast Path. There may be Dexter cattle grazing on the cliff tops, as the Coast Path is followed for a quarter mile towards the Point with its prominent cross.

3. Follow the delightful Coast Path, with the occasional kissing gate; at a junction there is a 'footpath to Penare' sign, providing a shorter return to the car park should this be desired. Otherwise, continue along the Coast Path, above Vault Beach. After a kissing gate go slightly uphill to another gate ('National Trust. Lamledra'), with Lamledra Farm in view. There is quite a long descent before the

Dodman Point

rise towards the farm. Go left at a fork below the farm to rise to a gate.

4. Turn left along a track, soon reaching another gate and the public road; there is a small car park to the left. Turn left for a prolonged but gentle ascent along the roadside, initially between high hedge banks but, after a gate, opening out with great coastal views.

5. At the next gate there is a choice; either continue along the road for a further 300m to a junction, turning left to return to Penare and the car park, or immediately before the gate, go over the stile on the left, cross a descending meadow to another stile, another meadow and a third stile to join the road close to the National Trust holiday cottage 'Bodrugan'. Turn left to walk along the road to the car park.

Walk 24: The Pentewan Railway Line

The Pentewan Railway was constructed by Sir Christopher Hawkins in 1829 to transport china clay from the St Austell area to the port at Pentewan, which had a lock connection to the sea. Coal and lime were imported, providing return freight to St Austell. The line was built to a gauge of two feet six inches and was never connected to the main railway system, which reached St Austell some years later. Although there were extensions to the port and reservoirs were constructed just inland of Pentewan, there was a constant (and losing) battle against silting. During the early years the loaded wagons travelled most of the way to the port by gravity; horses were used to complete the journey. In 1874 steam locomotives were introduced; there were never more than two at any one time. Although there was never an official passenger service on the line, the Hawkins family had a saloon carriage and occasional Sunday School outings used trucks to carry passengers to Pentewan.

The final freight was carried on the second of March 1918, following which the rails were lifted. However, at the port there were various branches to the quays, including one serving a small engine shed. Small sections of rail can still be found in situ.

Distance	4 km (2½ miles)
Ascent	None
Start/car parking	Layby on the B3273, St Austell to Mevagissey road, grid reference 008502. Opposite Queenie's General Store at London Apprentice. An alternative is a small off-road car park, accessed by a roadway to a quarry, a quarter mile south of the layby
Refreshments	Inn and café at Pentewan
Map	Ordnance Survey Explorer 105, Falmouth and Mevagissey, 1:25,000

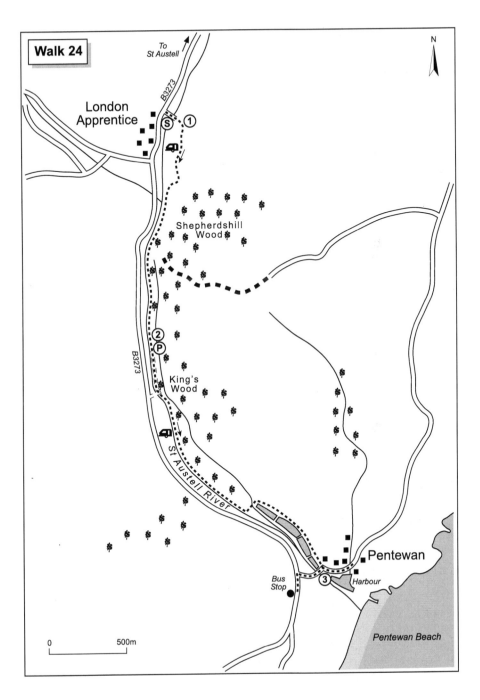

Unlike nearby Mevagissey, Pentewan is a comparatively quiet little resort of some charm, with inn, café and shop. There is access to a large adjacent beach.

The curiously named London Apprentice, with large caravan site, is nothing more than a straggle of houses and a general store, strung along the Mevagissey road, B3273.

The walk is very easy, the former railway line, now the 'Pentewan Trail' for horse riders, cyclists and walkers, providing much of the route, close to the St Austell River. King's Wood is an area of ancient woodland of native English trees, with its own system of organised footpaths.

The Pentewan to St Austell bus service provides the return for this linear walk.

The Walk

Walk to the St Austell end of the layby; turn right at once, at a 'Pentewan Valley Trail' signpost. Cross the river, bearing left then right; there are cycle trail signs.

1. In a further 20m turn right at another 'Pentewan Valley Trail signpost. More signs include 'Coast and Clay Trail'. The broad track passes behind a large caravan site, with a wooded valley side to the left and hedgerows rich in foxgloves and campion. At a signposted gate and barrier turn right, along a minor road, reaching a signpost and the small car park mentioned above, now on tarmac. At the next signposted junction turn right slightly downhill. The track is excellent, with King's Wood, rich in beech, sycamore and holly, to the left. Cross a stream and bear left, soon along a more open section, with the river and road to the right.

2. Pass another car park and a 'Welcome to King's Wood' information board. Continue between the former railway embankment and the river, passing the end of a wooden bridge. Go straight ahead – 'Pentewan one mile' – Across the river is another caravan site. Bear left into woodland; large areas of swampy ground are avoided by the excellent track. Cross a wooden bridge at a ford and pass a

Sea Lock, Pentewan

plaque recording the opening of the trail on the thirty-first of March 1995. Before joining the road in Pentewan, pass a cycle hire depot.

3. Turn left at the road to reach the village centre and harbour. An information board near the harbour includes interesting old photographs of village and railway. It is worth going a little further along the line of the former railway to find the sea lock, the loading quays and the embedded lengths of rail.

To return, go back to the main road. Cross the road, turn left and walk for fifty metres. Wait for the bus back to London Apprentice (26 or 526 – each is an hourly service) across the road from the bus shelter.

Walk 25: Looe and Kilminorth Woods

The busy fishing port of Looe has most of its town facilities such as inns, cafés, shops and museum on the east side of the harbour, with buildings climbing the steep hillside, not unlike some Mediterranean ports. It is an attractive place, probably seen at its best when there is fishing boat activity at the quayside.

East Looe is the terminus of the lovely little branch railway line from Liskeard.

On the far side of the harbour, West Looe is largely residential but has an enormous main car park on land beside the river, formerly the site of boatyards.

The thickly wooded slopes of the West Looe River comprise a local nature reserve with extensive public access, well-established tracks providing a choice of walking routes. One end of the woodland is adjacent to the major car park in West Looe; at the other end is the charming mini hamlet of Watergate. The views over the estuarial river are good and the bird life is rich and varied. The 'Giant's Hedge', high up the hillside, is believed to be a 6th century boundary dyke.

Use of the track which stays closest to the river provides an out and back route which qualifies as 'level' for the present purpose. A circular

Distance	5km (3 miles)
Ascent	80m (263ft)
Start/car parking	Vast pay and display car park at West Looe, entered a short distance above the bridge linking East and West Looe, grid reference 250538
Refreshments	Inns and cafés in Looe
Map	Ordnance Survey Explorer 107, St Austell and Liskeard, 1:25,000

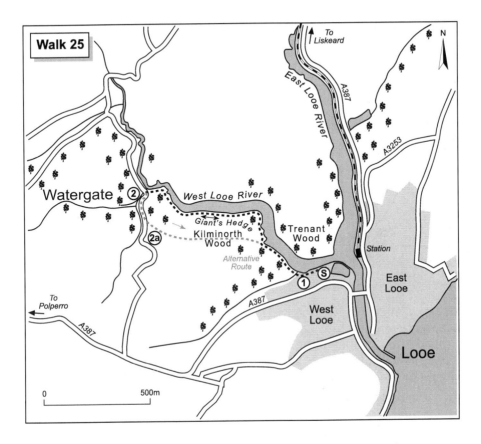

walk can be achieved but at the expense of greater ascent, as set out below.

The Walk

Head for the far end of the car park, passing a slipway.

1. Go through a gate, beside an information board. There are colour-coded routes through the woods. Follow a broad, hard-surfaced track keeping as close to the West Looe River as possible. After crossing a little bridge the track narrows; a signpost indicates steps up to the left for use at high tide, otherwise continue along the riverside beach. The path soon rises away from the water edge;

Looe

ignore any paths to the left, staying with the main path as it rises and falls gently across the hillside.

2. Go through a little gate to reach Watergate hamlet, close to the river at the foot of a cul de sac road. Retrace the route to return to the car park at Looe.

   Or, for a circular walk, turn left at Watergate to walk uphill along the road for approximately 300m. This adds a short amount to the length of the walk and, more importantly, about 30m (98ft) to the net overall ascent.

2a. Turn very sharp left to leave the road and go through a gate; there is a signpost 'bridleway Looe 1¹/₃ miles'. The excellent track stays high on the hillside. There are various signposted diversions but unless you want to explore the 'Giant's Hedge' ignore these, following 'Looe', straight ahead at all junctions. Go through a gate to rejoin the outward route fairly close to the point of entry to Kilminorth Woods, turning right to return to the car park.

Walk 26: Looe and Polperro

First, a warning. This walk, using a fine section of the South West Coast Path, is very much at the upper limit of what is acceptable for this book and many 'level' walkers will read no further. Having said that, the lure of walking from a fine port such as Looe to the iconic fishing village of Polperro, with the convenient linkage of the 573 bus, could well prove to be irresistible for those willing and able to make the extra effort.

Looe is described briefly in walk 25.

Polperro ranks highly among Cornwall's 'must see' villages; an atmospheric jumble of predominantly old buildings improbably crammed into the narrow space at the back of a tiny cove and harbour between high headlands. Immensely popular, the village is bustling for much of the year. Fortunately, vehicular access to the narrow streets is restricted, with large parking areas half a mile inland intercepting the great majority. Apart from a beach, Polperro has everything for visitors, including a small museum.

Distance	7¼km (4½ miles). Add 1½km (1 mile) for a start from the main car park in Looe
Ascent	Approximately 130m (427ft). Add 20m (66ft) for a start from the main car park in Looe
Start/car parking	Extensive parking on a long section of road at Hannafore Point, reached from West Looe, grid reference 255523
Refreshments	Abundant choice in Looe and Polperro. Smugglers' Rest, licensed café at Talland. Talland Bay Beach Café (seasonal)
Map	Ordnance Survey Explorer 107, St Austell and Liskeard, 1:25,000

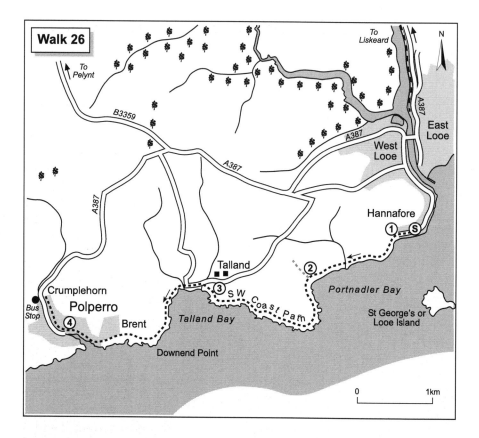

With the usual ups and downs of the coast path, the walk is quite demanding but there are no difficulties underfoot.

There is an hourly bus service (573) between Looe and Polperro, but the greatest advantage (saving half a mile of road walking and considerable ascent) is gained by parking close to Hannafore Point to start the walk, with the return from Polperro on the 573 bus which turns right at West Looe to go along the road to Hannafore Point, from where it circles back to West, then East Looe. This variation of the 573 route is used by alternate buses; i.e. one every two hours.

Another advantage at the end of the walk is the use of the (electric) 'Polperro Tram', running frequently between the inland edge of the harbour village, up the steadily rising road, to the bus terminus close to the lower end of the car park, opposite the Crumplehorn Inn.

The Walk

Start by walking to the far end of the cul de sac road at Hannafore.

1. Go through a signposted 'Talland Bay 3 miles, coast path' kissing gate and follow the path over grass, with great views of St George's (Looe) Island. Cross a tiny stream and go through more kissing gates. At an apparent fork keep left. Cross a stream on a bridge and pass a National Trust 'Hendersick' sign. Go up a long flight of steps, the first significant ascent of the walk. Rise again to reach a waymaked post at a junction.

2. Continue along the coast path, straight ahead, for 'Polperro 2¾ miles'. Gorse is the dominant vegetation for much of this route but with an array of wild flowers, particularly in Spring. There are more

Polperro

gates, more rises and a seat with great views. Go down a flight of steps, then rise again before Talland Bay comes into view. Leave the National Trust property, go down steps, soon descending gently to the back of Talland Bay. On the far side of the bay Downend Point is rugged, apparently blocking the way to Polperro. There are more steps before the path heads for a minor road above a stony little beach. To the right is the Smugglers' Rest, licensed café.

3. Join the road by a signpost, turning left, then left again, to walk past public conveniences to the small beach and the Talland Bay

Beach Café. There are several signposts, with estimates of the mileages to Looe and to Polperro. Continue, turning left at a waymarked T-junction to start a brutally steep but not too long ascent. Turn left part way up the ascent at a waymarked post, go up a few steps and follow the coast path, on tarmac towards an isolated house, West Cliff Old Court. Pass below the house and a National Trust 'Talland Cliffs' sign. The estimated '2 miles' to Polperro is inaccurate. A long rising section

Horse bus, Polperro

of path heads for a cross, the Polperro War Memorial, on the skyline. Pass the memorial, rising a little further before commencing the descent towards Polperro. The mouth of the harbour comes into view and the way is never in doubt, bearing right to pass above the harbour wall and the small Polperro museum.

4. Continue along the main street, rising gently towards the car parking area at Crumplehorn, half a mile from the harbour. Facing the car park entrance, the bus stop is a short distance along the road to the left. Note there is a frequent service of electric powered 'Polperro Trams' and a horse drawn bus shuttling to and from Polperro village.

Walk 27: Siblyback Lake

Hardly one of Cornwall's major visitor attractions, anyone could be forgiven for not knowing about Siblyback Lake, a reservoir of modest size (140 acres) tucked away to the north of Liskeard, on the fringe of Bodmin Moor. Completed in 1967 and designated as a water park, the lake is quite charming, with attractive surroundings and some leisure facilities including a children's play area, a sailing centre, a bird hide and angling. There is a (seasonal) tea room and gift shop.

The circuit of the lake provides a good level walk with some mud as the only likely problem.

Walking at Siblyback Lake

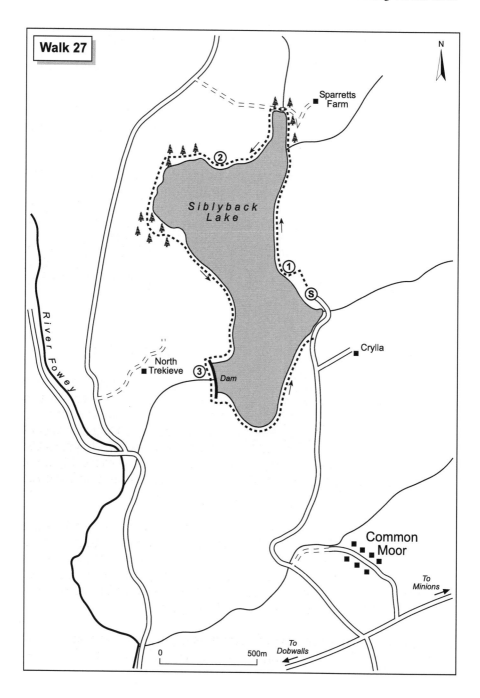

Walk 27

N

Sparretts
Farm

Siblyback
Lake

River Fowey

North
Trekieve

Dam

Crylla

Common
Moor

To
Minions

0   500m

To
Dobwalls

Distance	5km (3 miles)
Ascent	Negligible
Start/car parking	Pay and display car park with public conveniences at the water park, grid reference 236708. From Liskeard head north on B3254, passing St Cleer before going (almost) straight across a more major road to head for Siblyback Water Park along a signposted lane
Refreshments	Tea shop at water park (Easter to autumn)
Map	Ordnance Survey Explorer 109, Bodmin Moor, 1:25,000

The Walk

Walk past the tea shop, bearing left towards the lake shore.

1. At the shore turn right to follow a fine path, initially over grass. Go through a little gate with a notice warning of rugged terrain and the need for stout footwear. Pass through bracken before reaching a patch of woodland, with a bridge over a stream. Outbuildings of Sparretts Farm are to the right as the path bears left, to cross the marshy area at the head of the lake. Cross a small footbridge; the area is rich in bramble and this end of the lake seems to have the greatest attraction for large flocks of water fowl.

2. An area of coniferous woodland is entered at a boardwalk. Despite several more boardwalks, this wooded area is likely to be muddy as the path threads its way through. After an open section, pass through another area of coniferous woodland, again with the aid of boardwalks across the muddiest patches. Rise a little to reach the near end of the dam, a considerable structure.

3. Turn left to cross the top of the dam on a good walkway, with views down the valley to the right. At the far end go through a gate,

turning left to continue across a small picnic area, soon reaching the Siblyback access road at a gate. Turn left and cross a stream before turning left again to rise gently to the parking area.

Siblyback Lake

Walk 28: Minions and the Cheesewring

Bodmin Moor is one of the great granite uplands of the West Country, rich in stone circles, standing stones and other monuments, largely of the late Bronze/early Iron Ages, when the relatively benign climate permitted some primitive farming. This ancient landscape has long yielded tin and other minerals and, in the 19th century, its fine building stone was extensively quarried.

The Hurlers comprises three adjacent Bronze Age stone circles, whilst the Cheesewring is the finest of several similar examples of the result of prolonged weathering by wind and water on the softer rocks which formerly surrounded the now exposed cores of very hard granite. Not surprisingly, legends have grown concerning druids and magic golden cups at this potentially mystic site. Early in the 19th century a golden cup was, in fact, found with a skeleton in a nearby burial chamber. Ownership of the cup passed to the Royal family; according to different accounts the late King George V used it either as an ash tray or as a receptacle for his collar studs.

The adjacent Cheesewring Quarry was large and highly productive of good quality stone, used for many major structures, including London's Tower Bridge and Westminster Bridge. Stone was taken from this and from other quarries in the area by a long tramway to Moorswater, near Liskeard, for onward transit to Looe by canal and,

Distance	5½km (3½ miles)
Ascent	55m (181ft), not including the steep little ascent to the Cheesewring
Start/car parking	Car park at the north-east end of Minions, grid reference 261712
Refreshments	Tea shops in Minions
Map	Ordnance Survey Explorer 109, Bodmin Moor, 1:25,000

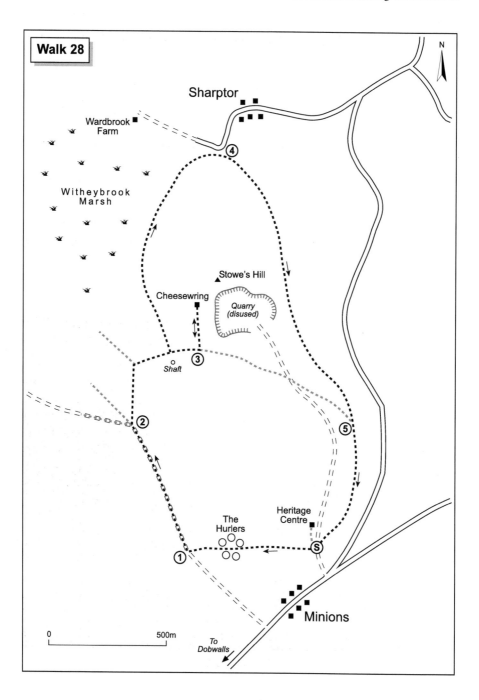

Walk 28

Sharptor

Wardbrook
Farm

Witheybrook
Marsh

Stowe's Hill ▲

Cheesewring

*Quarry
(disused)*

○ *Shaft*

③

②

⑤

The
Hurlers

Heritage
Centre

①

Ⓢ

Minions

0   500m

*To
Dobwalls*

N

from 1859, by railway; most of the granite slabs used to anchor the rails are still in situ.

Daniel Gumb was an 18th century mathematician who worked as a stonecutter. He lived with his wife and family in a house/cave, close to the present quarry. The dwelling has been partly reconstructed.

Windswept Minions, claiming to be the highest village in Cornwall, is hardly pretty but does have tea shops and a heritage centre which is located in the engine house of a former mine just outside the village. Despite the overall ruggedness of Bodmin Moor, this is an easy walk, with no serious ascent. After visiting the Cheesewring the path used for the full walk is rather vague for rather more than half a mile, but the overall direction is clear and there is no difficulty underfoot. Care is required for the short ascent to the Cheesewring.

The Walk

From the signpost at the top left corner of the car park follow 'The Hurlers'. Above, to the right, is the former engine house, now Minions

The Hurlers

Heritage Centre. Go straight across a broad track and walk along a grassy path leading directly to the celebrated stone circles. After the circles continue in the same direction for about 200m to reach a broad, stony, track. The Pipers standing stones are close to the track.

1. Turn right here to follow the track, rising gently, with tors including the Cheesewring visible ahead to the right. There are tracks to the left leading to other Bronze Age features and to former quarries.

2. At a three-way junction bear right to head towards the Cheesewring, descending gently to cross a shallow valley. Rise up the far side of the valley, passing close to the top of a fenced-off mining shaft.

3. At a junction near the top of the rise, a broad grass track forks to the left to provide a route for those wishing to see the rock tors at

The Cheesewring

close quarters and with a view into the former Cheesewring Quarry. Above the grass track there are various little rocky paths leading to the top. Follow the fence above the quarry. With or without the ascent to the Cheesewring there is a choice here.

For a shorter walk continue along the main path, over a low summit before descending to rejoin the full route at point 5.

For the full walk retrace the route by descending towards the main path and the shallow valley. Daniel Gumb's Cave can be found by making a short detour to the left, towards the quarry, well before returning to the main path. Some distance before reaching the valley bottom on the main path, turn right along a fairly clear path, almost opposite the fenced-off shaft top. There are scattered thorn bushes to the right. Pass below the bushes to continue along the side of Stowe's Hill; the path is not always clear but the walking surface is good and the route is level. Wardbrook Farm comes in to view ahead; the path bends to the right to pass approximately 200m above the farm. The rock-strewn Sharp Tor is now ahead and the route joins a surfaced farm access road at a gate.

4. Do not go along the road; follow a narrow but clear path to the right of the roadside fence, soon reaching the granite blocks on the line of the former mineral tramway. This tramway provides an entirely certain route back to Minions. Cheesewring Farm is below to the left as long views open up to the east and north-east, including the village of Henwood. The communications mast on Caradon Hill comes into view ahead, with the Cheesewring tors now above to the right and the huge quarry spoil heaps adjacent.

5. There is a stone wall close on the left as a track (the short cut) joins from the right. At a fork stay with the tramway. At the next fork, with four large boulders, bear right towards the former engine house, rising gently. Turn left to return to the car park.

Also from Sigma Leisure:

Best Tea Shop Walks in the Isle of Wight
Jacqui Leigh

The Isle of Wight is a wonderful place to walk with 500 miles of footpaths, the highest footpath density in the UK, and numerous teashops in beautiful locations. The walks in this book vary in length and difficulty; some include at least part suitable for wheelchair users or pushchairs, giving the option of 'there and back' walks. The teashops range from the very tradition to modern cafe style establishments.
£8.99

Walking with Kids
Games and activities to make walking fun
Angela Youngman

Going for a walk can be great fun, educational and healthy. This book offers games and activities introducing kids to the environment whilst walking include tracking, looking for signs of changing seasons, mini beast hunting, feather collecting and art and craft activities in woods, forests, open country, rivers, seaside, towns and evening walks.
£8.99

Best Tea Shop Walks in Kent
Norman and June Buckley

28 circular walks in the 'Garden of England' — all easily accessed from such major centres as Sevenoaks, Maidstone, Dove, Folkestone and Canterbury — are suitable for all the family. Favourite areas such as the North Downs and the Weald feature strongly, but coverage is comprehensive with walks based on attractive towns and villages throughout Kent. Each walk includes at least one personally tried-and-tested 'walker friendly' tea shop.
£6.95

The Charlie Chaplin Walk
Steven P Smith

The Charlie Chaplin Walk is targeted at fans of Chaplin, those interested in film history, people with a connection to the Lambeth and Kennington areas of London and anybody with an interest of the social history of London's poor of the late Victorian and early Edwardian era.

Explore the London streets of Charlie Chaplin's childhood in a chronological tour that can be taken on foot or from the comfort of an armchair. This book concentrates on the story of Chaplin's formative years and takes a fresh look at the influence they had upon his films.
£9.99

Traditional Derbyshire Fare
300 recipes plus the stories and anecdotes behind them
Jill Armitage

Some Derbyshire dishes are well known, like the Bakewell Pudding; many more, including some of the most delectable, are little known outside the places whose name they bear. The recipes are individual, easy, economical, with readily available ingredients, and have a strong regional accent. This is Derbyshire food at its best.
£12.99

A Calendar of Cotswold Cookery
June Lewis-Jones

Enjoy a feast that is a true taste of the Cotswolds. A superb treat combining history, legend, folklore — and food. This cookery book brings together hundreds of traditional recipes, which the author has scoured from the region from Bath to Chipping Campden in her quest for the dishes that make Cotswold cookery so special.
£12.99

Peak District Walking
On The Level
Norman Buckley

This is a book for people who enjoy a relaxed approach to walking — walks that can be enjoyed whatever the weather. The walks are ideal for family outings and the precise instructions ensure that ther's little chance of losing your way. Well produced maps and inviting photographs encourage everyone to try out the walks. The whole of the Peak District is covered — both the Dark Peak and the White Peak — with visits to such gems as Edale, Castleton, Eyam, Chatsworth and Bakewell.
£6.95

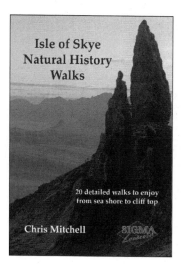

Isle of Skye Natural History Walks
20 detailed walks to enjoy from sea shore to cliff top
Christopher Mitchell

An alternative guide to the wildlife and geology of Skye detailing where to see the island's lesser-known natural history. There are 20 walks based around Portree, Dunvegan, Broadford and Sleat together with detailed maps and quality photographs. Skye has long been regarded as a special place for the birdwatcher, the geologist, the botanist and marine biologist. By taking time to 'stand and stare' you will discover for yourself this hidden side of Skye – one that complements the traditional image of seascapes and mountain views.
£9.99

More Lakeland Walking
On the Level 2nd Edition
Norman Buckley

A newly revised and updated edition of the follow-up to Norman Buckley's extremely successful Lakeland Walking on the Level, it adds a further 27 Lakeland walks which combine minimum effort with maximum pleasure. The walks are all circular and start and finish at a recommended parking area. Some are among the high mountains of the Lake District, whilst others explore the often neglected but attractive fringe areas.
£8.99

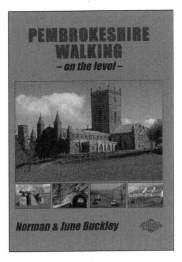

Pembrokeshire Walking
On the level
Norman & June Buckley

This is the sixth volume of the popular and well-establsihed series of 'level walks' books. Discover both the breath-taking splendour of the Pembrokeshire coast and its diverse inland landscape. The 25 comparatively short, easy walks in this book include clear route directions, map and a brief description of features encountered along the way as well as recommendations for refreshment.
£8.99

Walking in the Footsteps of Robin Hood
in Nottinghamshire
Jill Armitage

Walking in the Footsteps of Robin Hood roots out the places mentioned in traditional old tales and visits the locations that Robin and his men would have known. Walk through some of middle England's finest countryside on miles of well-marked footpaths to interesting historical sites associated with the outlaw legend. Stoops, caves, wells and stones with the outlaws names have been traced and woven into the walks taking you through Robin Hood country.

£8.99

Country Walks in and around Warwickshire
Ron Weston

This selection of 32 Warwickshire walks takes you on a journey of picturesque villages and historic churches, stately homes and castles, famous gardens and medieval tracks bound together by a superb network of public footpaths and canal towpaths and sometimes spilling over into adjoining counties. All walks in the book are circular, the longest being 5½ miles and all within a radius of 25 miles from Coventry, with directions of how to get there and where to park.

£8.99

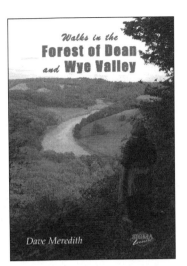
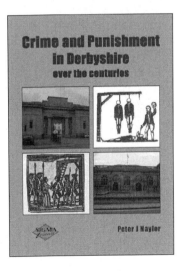